Merry Chr~ W9-BKC-978

2003

To: Nicole and Will

From: Aunt Jayce

EGGSTRA COURAGE
FOR THE
CHICKEN HEARTED

More Heartfelt Stories to
Encourage Confident Living

by

Becky Freeman
Susan Duke
Rebecca Barlow Jordan
Gracie Malone
Fran Caffey Sandin

CARMEL • NEW YORK 10512

www.guideposts.org

Eggstra Courage for the Chicken Hearted:
More Heartfelt Stories to Encourage Confident Living
ISBN 1-56292-599-7
Copyright © 1999 by Becky Freeman, Susan Duke, Rebecca Barlow Jordan, Gracie Malone, Fran Caffey Sandin
P.O. Box 323
Quinlan, Texas 75474

This Guideposts edition is published by special arrangement with Honor Books.

ACKNOWLEDGMENTS

First of all, the Hens want to chirp the praises of our editor at Honor Books, Rebecca Currington. She truly is the honorary "Queen of our Writing Coop."

In addition, we want to thank all the folks at Honor Books who have believed in our project, prayed for our efforts, pampered us with thoughtful gifts and gestures of kindness, and worked diligently to get these words of encouragement into the hands of those hungry for a little good news.

We want to thank the patient roosters and chicks in our family nests who—though they sometimes laugh at our crazy sisterhood of henship—always believed we could fly.

To our readers who made our first book a soaring success, how we appreciate your encouragement. It is the grain we feed on!

Finally, to the One Who covers us with His loving wings as we waddle through this life. Lord, we know without You, we'd have nothing of substance to say, no reason to look up and laugh for joy. You are our life.

With grins,

The Hens with Pens

DEDICATION

To the Roosters, Chicks and Grandchicks
who feather our nests
with love and encouragement.

INTRODUCTION

Return of the Big Chickens!

It's been a year since we Hens with Pens pecked out our last book, *Courage for the Chicken Hearted*. Since that time, we've met hundreds of fellow hens who are waddling and strutting toward courage, faith, and a life of joy and laughter. Even though life is not always easy, and each of us chicks had our moments of tears—all in all, we have to admit: we've had more fun in our crazy coop than ought to be legal.

We only wish we could gather all our reader friends into our writing nest for a personal visit. There's nothing like an afternoon of nestling around Gracie's "Mother Hen" hearth while we munch on Fran's yummy brownies, hear the latest funny antic from Becky, a tale of compassion from Suzie, or a word of spiritual refreshment from Rebecca.

We hope this book will allow you the next best thing to a real visit to our hen pen. May these freshly pecked stories give you a "virtual visit" filled with moments of love, laughter, and inspiration. We'd like to encourage you to start your own perpetual hen party with a few friends who are dedicated to a life of love and encouragement.

Since all of us have days when the sky seems to be falling, it is imperative that we hens have friends who will gather 'round us, believe in us, love us, and pray for us. If these stories inspire even one lone ranger chicken to join a hen pen of nurturing friends who'll inspire her to growth, we will have accomplished our purpose.

Now enough of our cackling. It's time to snuggle into your favorite nesting place and crack open a few good stories. May you feel the presence of God's loving wings around you as you read, as we so often did when we wrote.

Becky Freeman
Susan Duke
Rebecca Barlow Jordan
Gracie Malone
Fran Caffey Sandin

TABLE OF CONTENTS

Section I
Life in the Henhouse
Courage in Family Relationships

Section II
Just among Hens
Courage in Nurturing Friendships

Section III
Chickens on Parade
Courage When Celebrating Life's Special Moments

Section IV
Winging It One Day at a Time
Courage When Facing a Crisis—Big or Small

Section V
Spreading Your Wings
Courage for Growing Closer to God

SECTION I

Life in the Henhouse

Courage in Family Relationships

CHAPTER 1

Handy Dandy Rooster Repairs

by Fran Caffey Sandin

One day while shopping for household items, I spied a padded potty seat. Remembering our ancient bathroom with the cracked and peeling lid, I thought . . . *hey, we need one of those.* So after propitiously pondering the proper decision, I purchased the pink one with embroidered flowers on the lid and hurried home.

Eager to see my new "touch of class" in place, I carried it in from the car, grabbed a small wrench, and skipped toward our bathroom to detach the old lid.

Kneeling beside the commode, I tried to unscrew the metal bolts. The left screw rotated 'round and 'round, but the bolt never loosened. Then I sat on the floor straddling the bowl, awkwardly hugging it as I reached around, straining to unscrew the left and then the right. Nothing happened. My farm-girl experiences had prepared me to tackle all kinds of fix-it problems from vacuum cleaner repairs to assembling furniture. But the hefty potty seat would not budge, so I asked my handy dandy rooster repairman to flex his muscles and give me a hand. After all, my urologist hubby was sort of a plumber anyway.

"Show me the new potty seat and I'll be glad to put it on," Jim agreed brightly, flashing his confident Superman smile. Sensing that "he-men" need room to work, I stepped into the next room to fold clothes.

At first I heard nothing but a little scooting about and Jim's cheerful whistling. A minute or two later, however, his whistling was punctuated by a few groans and "ughs." Then Jim darted to the garage for a screwdriver. After more clanking and grunting, he headed for the garage again and reappeared with a larger tool. His face was as red as a rooster's comb, and I was beginning to worry.

"Are you having a little trouble, dear?" I asked sheepishly.

"Oh, you know how these old metal bolts are—both are frozen in place."

Soon he began beating metal against metal to loosen the bolts before trying again to unscrew them. Jim struggled and tugged about half an hour before announcing, "I'm taking a break."

While he rested in the den, I had an idea. Perhaps he had loosened the bolts enough that I could waltz in, unscrew the old, put on the new, and surprise him. Surveying the situation, I noticed that dirt particles had fallen into the water. Without thinking, I reached up to flush the commode. As soon as my hand left the handle, I knew I'd made a terrible mistake. A geyser the size of "Old Faithful" spurted out the side of the bowl. "Jim, help!" I yelled, jumping back away from the spray.

"Hey, what are you doing? What happened? Let me through so I can turn off the water," Jim shouted, rushing by me and reaching below the stool for the turn-off valve. Then I saw the panicked look in his eyes as it dawned on him that our old plumbing did not include one.

The water level continued to rise as Jim raced to the garage to find the long-handled rod for cutting off the water main in front of the house. Then he had to dig a hole in the flower bed to get to it. In the meantime, I pulled the towels off the racks and used them as sandbags to keep the water from flooding the adjoining bedrooms. Then I attempted to scoop up some of the water and pour it into the shower stall with a small cleaning bucket I found under the sink.

The only nice thing about that Saturday was the bright sunshine outside. Everything inside went downhill fast. Once the water had been turned off, we examined the wreckage and discovered that the porcelain stool was cracked. We had no choice but to replace the entire fixture. Oh, the joys of home ownership!

Jim, normally a happy guy, took on the demeanor of a bulldog while I searched the bookshelf for *Will This Marriage Survive?* After numerous growls and three more trips to the hardware store, Jim, with steam emanating from his ears, successfully installed a new commode, a turn-off valve, a new main cut-off valve, and my new potty seat. (By the way, it's lovely.)

Realizing that my husband had spent his entire day off on this simple project, I apologized for the trouble I'd caused, crowned him "My Hero," and baked a batch of his favorite Deer Valley Cowboy Cookies.

Last Christmas, we had a kind of encore. A few minutes before our company was to arrive, I decided to tidy up the utility bathroom. When I flushed the commode, it kept running, running, and running. Then water began spilling over the top. I frantically jiggled the handle to no avail, and then, lifted the tank lid. Imagine my astonishment as a powerful stream of water hit the ceiling and showered back down on my head. Reaching inside the tank, I located the broken metal part and held my hand over it to stop the flow. I felt about as desperate as the Dutch boy with his finger in the dike.

That's when I spotted a turn-off valve near the baseboard. So I stuffed a towel in the tank and tried with all my strength to turn the valve. It seemed welded into place. Plunging in another towel as reinforcement, I raced to the garage for the pipe wrench and applied that to the stubborn valve, but despite my twists and turns, it would not budge.

Jim was running errands in town so I beeped him. When he called from his car phone, I cried, "Jim, our commode in the utility room just blew up. Water is flying everywhere and I can't fix it!" Knowing what he would ask, I added, "I can't turn off the valve."

"I'm on my way home," he said calmly, "but in the meantime, call the plumber."

So at 4:00 P.M. on December 23, I phoned a local plumber, who said that if I would go and buy a new commode, he would come by and install it. "I'm in a hurry," he stressed. "Go shopping right away."

A few minutes later, our daughter, son-in-law, and granddaughter drove in the back driveway and entered through the open back door. When they walked around the corner, they stopped short. There I was (peering through my new string-mop hairdo, mascara dripping down my face) standing over the commode with both hands in the tank, trying to control Niagara Falls. I briefly explained the situation to them as Jim arrived. We placed a brick over the leak, turned off the main water valve, and hurried off to the store.

He and I were laughing as we drove to the lumberyard just before closing time to buy another Christmas present for each other. Jim was in such a jovial mood, I asked him to make the selection. He decided in thirty seconds, and without debate, I said, "We'll take it."

After the plumbers, Billy and Dale, had removed the old fixture and replaced it with the new, Billy stood back and gazed at his handiwork. "You know Dale, that toilet for the handicapped looks real nice in here. I think I'll get me one of them."

Jim and I looked at each other and gasped. "A potty for the handicapped?"

"Oh, yes Ma'am," he said. "This is one of those *real high* ones."

"My six-foot, four-inch husband thinks it's perfect," I said, smiling, "but the rest of us may need a ladder." I quickly placed greenery and a big red bow on top for decoration and thanked the plumbers for rescuing us from the flood.

Looking back, I can better see the value of situations like these. Through them, Jim and I learned to be more flexible and not take everything so seriously, including our plumbing problems. After all, life is full of unpredictable events. We've also learned a few other things—like the value of kindness, and most of all, the unmeasureable worth of a good sense of humor.

A happy face means a glad heart.
Proverbs 15:13 TLB

Chicken Nugget

A Booster for the Rooster
(Ten Tips for Encouraging Your Husband)

1. Pray for him daily.
2. Look into his eyes when he is speaking.
3. Stay physically attractive—and tell him how good looking he is, too!
4. Be flexible—willing to put down what you are doing, if at all possible, in order to focus on him.
5. Leave a snack on the table for him when he works late.
6. Stay mentally alert and share information you've learned.
7. Arrange for special date nights or weekend getaways.
8. Be trustworthy with finances.
9. Be supportive of your husband in public— eager for his success.
10. Encourage him with Scripture verses, a special quote written on a card, or even a funny cartoon. Leave them on his desk, mirror, or the dashboard of his car.

CHAPTER 2

Cheap, Cheap, Cheap

by Rebecca Barlow Jordan

"That's suicide to your ministry!" friends said when Larry resigned his Arizona pastorate with no other prospects in mind.

I remember well the morning my husband laid this surprise announcement egg and rolled it in my direction. Lying beside me, Larry looked into my eyes, as if searching for some haven of understanding. "Honey, I think I've completed my ministry here. I've been praying about this for some time. How would you feel if I resigned in a couple of months?"

My calm response surprised even me. I thought of Valerie, our oldest child, who would graduate from high school in two years. Then of our younger daughter, Jennifer, who would enter middle school in the fall. Finally, I thought, *Although Arizona was not my "hatching" place, for twelve years now it had been my "nesting" place.*

My parents lived only forty miles away. My girlfriends and I had strolled our babies through these palm tree-lined neighborhoods. Together we'd launched our "Proverbs 31 Woman" ventures—from making sun-dried raisins (mine always blew away into the wild blue yonder) to canning fresh peach jam. In Bible studies and kitchen-table talks, we had exhorted each other through motherhood's highest joys and deepest traumas. My roots had grown deep in this Arizona soil.

Just the same, I had to admit that inside my heart, I'd been experiencing, in Shakespearean terms, "the winter of my discontent." I longed for a fresh touch from God.

It must have been God's preparation—the unrest in my spirit—that helped me respond to Larry: "Whatever you feel is best. Honey, somehow, I know God will provide." They were noble words. But did I really believe them? The next few months would tell.

Larry's resignation rocked the church. As a barrage of questions kept coming our way, "Why? Why? Why?" I resisted the urge to say, "No, Larry didn't duck out with the church funds. No, he isn't experiencing burnout or mid-life crisis. No, he wasn't forced to leave." These were the three most popular explanations for a quick pulpit exodus, but none of them fit our situation. It just seemed to be God's timing.

The church generously gave us three accumulated weeks of vacation pay, as well as five weeks of unused sabbatical pay, leaving us with eight weeks to figure out the next step. That afforded a bit of security, certainly generous on the part of the church, but it was still an awakening to realize that in eight short weeks that security would vanish.

When Larry suggested ever so gently, "Honey, why don't you write out your skills? You may need to work for awhile," my hidden fears floated to the surface as reality sank to the bottom of my heart.

I'm willing to move away from my nest, I fussed at the Lord. *Do I also have to fly into an unemployment line? Doesn't Larry realize that I feel CALLED to stay at home?* Then I offered God an alternate plan. *Lord, I'm a big coupon clipper. I can be the Chief Chick of Cheap, Cheap, Cheap, and we can make ends meet without having to resort to a briefcase!*

Then I realized the real reason for my stubbornness. This mother hen was a boneless chicken with few job skills to feather her talentless cap.

Reluctantly, I grabbed my pen and began to wrack my scrambled brain for some potential wage-earning abilities. The longer I sat, the more I realized I couldn't even lay one egg of an idea. As soon as I felt the slightest stirring of inspiration, I scratched it off as hopeless.

Hmmmm, let's see . . .

Degrees? Well, yes, I did get my official P.H.T. degree (putting hubby through school, that is). Unfortunately, most employers would not allow me to write my husband's degree in the blank beside "education."

Cooking—I agreed with Mamie McCullough who said, "When my kids ask for a hot breakfast, I microwave their Fruit Loops."

Cleaning—After kids were born, I christened my homes, "Desert Storm" or "Hurricane Andrew." Martha Stewart I am not.

Writing—Ah, yes, my heart's desire! But at that time my newspaper column and other writings combined would hardly pay for one chicken wing, much less a month of groceries.

Keeping Kids—With my history of PMS, this could be dangerous.

Signing—As a deaf interpreter for ten years, my fingers had flown as fast as anyone could preach. However, I was unemployable because I was not "certified" (though I have sometimes been called "certifiable").

Marketing—My talented girlfriend and I had carted our crafty wares to Christmas boutiques for years. It was a cash and carry operation. Every year I carried my wares back home again, while Millie cashed the checks from her sellout.

Secretarial skills—My best bet. What I did in the "B.C." days (before computers—and before children). But twelve years had passed since I worked in that capacity.

Throughout that eight-week "wilderness wandering," well-meaning friends kept voicing their curiosity: "What are you going to do? Are you moving away? Do you know where you'll go?"

"No, but God knows," I would answer with an air of confidence. Then reaching to heaven for childlike reassurance, I'd pray, *You do know what You're doing, don't You, Lord?*

Every morning we'd begin the day by asking the Lord for direction. Every evening we'd go off to bed with nothing new to report. Larry explored teaching possibilities at a nearby Bible college. Friends in the ministry agreed to recommend him if any church positions opened.

Slowly God softened my heart, and in spite of my lack of "credentials," I began to feel more confidence. I had no idea where this road would lead, but we called it our faith journey.

Admittedly, my prayers bordered on selfishness, "God, would You lead us someplace really beautiful—near mountains like Colorado, or maybe San Diego beaches? How about a resort ministry?" I never spoke it verbally, but silently I'd think, *Anywhere but Texas, Lord.* I'd lived in that big, barren land where the buffalo roamed, and the tumbleweeds blew where trees once stood. How could I nest again where the trees rolled away with the wind?

We struggled to understand, and yet, I must say this: At no time before, and at no time since, have we felt such peace about the future—and our hope was not in vain.

We have petitioned the Lord often in our ministry, and God answers, but not always in the nick of time. Early in our marriage, a job promised to me was given to someone else, and we were left to start graduate school with a meager thirty-five dollars a week country-church salary and a diet of fifteen-cent hamburgers.

But this time, our God, Who does all things well, Whose ways are greater than our ways, Whose thoughts far surpass our own, and Who loves to pour out His goodness on the undeserving, decided to bless a struggling family and answer far beyond what we could ask or imagine or hope. Our eight-week pay ended on Friday, September 14. On Monday, September 17, Larry walked into his new church office to begin his job as associate pastor.

Our love for the Lord, as a couple—and as a family—grew deeper and richer as the trauma of the move faded. As it turned out, every family member at that time needed a change. A few weeks before our move, I received a phone call from a publishing company in a suburb called Allen, offering me some assignments I could do at home. This was the beginning of a long and satisfying writing relationship. (Three "cheaps" for me!) And here's the interesting part: It was in the same town where Larry's ministry opportunity happened to open up. That's right, God moved us back to the land of denim, boots, and Southfork Ranch.

It's been more than ten years since that move, and we've nested and roosted and pecked ourselves deep into the heart of Texas, but I've yet to see one tumbleweed blow by my kitchen window. As a matter of fact, the foliage is green here in our East Texas neighborhood, and the mockingbirds and bluebonnets are as pretty as the folks are friendly.

As we say down here, with a southern drawl, "God is good, all the time (though many natives pronounce it "tahm")—and all the time, God is good." Even to us faith-wobbling chickens.

*Now to him who is able to do immeasurably more
than all we ask or imagine, according to his power
that is at work within us, to him be glory . . .
in Christ Jesus . . . for ever and ever!*
Ephesians 3:20,21

Chicken Nugget

Mail Manna from Heaven

To work or not to work?
That is the question.
Whether it's nobler to stay home
and fight the spiraling economy,
mother the troops, and bandage the
wounded, or enter the fierce battle
and attack the enemy with a head-on
offensive. Oh, who will deliver me from
this traumatic dilemma? Who will
appease my guilt if I stay? Yea, Lord,
You have seen my affliction and have
answered me in my time of need.
You have sent an angel in disguise,
with a postponement to decide.
Your heavenly mail manna has
provided an unexpected check again.

CHAPTER 3

As the Coop Turns

by Susan Duke

Only the Bible has produced more "begets" than my family tree. My husband, Harvey, is still trying to figure out the whole brood after all our years of marriage! I told him he might as well give up, because I'm still not quite sure myself.

It's a scary thing when you accidentally tune in to a soap opera and suddenly have an uncontrollable desire to pick up the phone, call the station, and say, "I've got better material than this on my worst day!" There are enough high-action drama stories and colorful characters in my family to keep a soap scriptwriter busy for years! I can hear it now, "Stay tuned tomorrow for another episode of 'As the Coop Turns.'"

When my mama married my daddy, she was sixteen, and he was a widower with four young children: Horace, Wynona, Pat, and Wink (a nickname for Winfred). My parents then proceeded to hatch five more children, Carroll (Bubba), Donnie, Brenda, Maria, and me. Pat, the baby from the first flock, was fifteen when I was born. She took me under her sisterly wings and pretty much raised me before she left home and got married.

Those of us blessed to come from large families sometimes struggle to find our own identities. My sister, Brenda, used to say, "When I look in the mirror, I never know if I'm looking at myself or another member of the family!" While loving and respecting your part in a conglomerate coop, it takes courage to leap from the family perch to seek your own individuality.

Having to share a room with my sister, Maria, had its volatile moments. Feather-splitting episodes sometimes left me wondering if I'd survive each day's adventures. I loved critters of every kind . . . frogs, lizards, rabbits, and cats. She, on the other hand, was terrified of them, especially when one occasionally got loose in our room (accidentally of course)!

There were times when I felt like a rebel chicken—independent, determined, and challenged to try my own wings away from the nest. I spent a lot of time roosting up in trees where I would sometimes read an entire book before coming down. Other times, I'd dash to the cow barn where I'd made my own cozy retreat and clubhouse.

Even though private time was precious, I cherish the memories of growing up in a home filled to the rafters with siblings. I remember my sister, Pat, taking me to town with her; making mud pies with Judy, my same-aged niece; and peering for hours into our tall, wooden, floor-model radio, hoping to catch a glimpse of Elvis!

One Christmas, Daddy played Santa Claus, and I was sure I heard reindeer on the roof. I remember, at age four, how my two older brothers surprised me with a swing set bought with money they'd saved working at a local grocery store. There were many Easters when the whole church came to our house to hunt eggs. Family camping trips and Thanksgiving reunions were always fun times. My first attempt at cooking was in the kitchen with my sister, Maria, making chocolate treats we still jokingly call "dog food cookies." Our family had its share of adversity, but we had an even bigger share of acceptance, unconditional love, and memories.

I realize now, years later, the struggle for identity has been a common trait in families down through the ages. I'm reminded of my daughter's determination to find her own true self. When Kelly was a teenager, she squawked about the vacations we'd often combine with buying trips for my antique shop.

"Someday," she said, "I'll have my own home, and I'll never have to look at another antique! My house will be totally modern." You can imagine my surprise when, soon after she was married, Kelly came home to visit and began asking if I might be willing to part with some of my old baskets, quilts, and other antique things around my house. It wasn't long before her style for home decorating began to look strangely familiar.

Tonight, when Kelly called long-distance, I told her I was writing about family relationships and finding our place in life. "Do you have any words of wisdom you'd like to contribute?" I asked, waiting for her usual lighthearted chuckle.

She surprised me, responding candidly with words that landed like soft feathers in my heart. "You know, Mom, you could share about how I used to say I hated antiques, hated shopping for them, and said I'd never have one antique in my house. I always thought I wanted modern furniture, but now, I can't imagine having anything but a country home. And of course you know that Robert and I love to shop for antiques, just like you and I used to do. I guess I'm more like you than I ever wanted to admit."

I held back warm tears as Kelly went on to say, "You know, you spend half your life trying to find your place in the world, only to realize that you were right where you needed to be all the time—near to your mother's heart. I remember how you made every holiday and every birthday extra special, and now I want to make the same kind of wonderful memories for my children. I want Kara and Noah to experience traditions I loved from childhood, traditions that fashioned me into the wife and mom that I am today. It's my heritage." When I didn't say anything right away, Kelly asked curiously, "Mom, are you crying?"

"I guess so," I said softly. "It's just that you've never told me these things before."

"Well, I guess I just thought you always knew how I felt," Kelly replied.

Maybe, deep down, I did, but Kelly's words were like a gift gently laid at my heart's door.

It seems stepping stones down the heart's pathway always lead us home. Next week is Thanksgiving, and Harvey and I will be making our yearly pilgrimage to my hometown in East Texas for our traditional family gathering. We'll sit around the table, and I will look into the faces of those I hold most dear in all the world. We'll hold hands, giggle, cry, and share the blessing of the bond that keeps the coop turning and us rebel chickens coming home year after year. We'll be making another memory and starring in yet another episode of "As the Coop Turns."

Years may change our circumstances, but our family memories shape our identities. They are our heritage—and the bread and butter of our souls.

The memory of the righteous will be a blessing.
Proverbs 10:7

Chicken Nugget

"Where we love is home,
Home that our feet may leave,
but not our hearts."

Oliver Wendell Holmes

CHAPTER 4

Chicken 'n' Dumplins

by Becky Freeman

By far the biggest difference between my husband, Scott, and me is this: I have no athletic ability—at all—while Scott is naturally tall and thin, works out with weights, and runs for the sheer pleasure of it. He also stays in shape by building our home, a chronic project that has taken up the better part of the last seven or eight years.

Recently, Scott finished the second story but refused to build a set of stairs to it. When I questioned the wisdom of this decision, he informed me that stairs were for sissies and what he had in mind would constitute a bit of an obstacle course— a splendid opportunity for family fitness and fun. I argued that I liked being a sissy, but alas, to no avail.

Scott, being Chief Builder in charge, created three ways to get from one floor to the other. Choice Number One—mine—is the "lean-to ladder." Choice Number Two—preferred choice for the kids who literally come swinging into the breakfast room like Tarzan—is "the rope." Choice Number Three is Scott's "rock-climbing wall." Yes, my family is literally climbing the walls.

As one might imagine, I am not exactly a rock climbing kind of woman. I'm not even a jumping jack or jogging kind of gal. I'm short and—let's just say I'm currently reading my 1,789th diet book for the utter euphoria of imagining what I might look like if I ever did get in shape. If reading books about losing weight would somehow do the trick, I'd currently be the size of a coffee stirrer.

A while back, I lunched with three women friends—Linda, Lori, and Mimi. Whatever possessed me to accept an invitation to dine with three women whose combined weight is probably less than that of my salad plate, I'll never know. And predictably the conversation soon turned to weight control. Linda began her pep talk.

"Becky, you've got to start running. I feel so great about myself since I've started jogging—it's unbelievable." Mimi nodded in agreement, "Yes, it's given me a real feeling of power." She paused to flex her beautifully tanned biceps and added, "We are woman, hear us roar!"

With so much energy surging in the atmosphere around me, I suddenly had the overpowering urge to take a nap. *I am woman, hear me snore.*

Though Lori, who is about the size of a trim gnat, had been quiet throughout the cheerleading session, I knew she shared my distaste for habitual exercise. And sure enough, when Linda complained that she hated to take off two weeks from her running schedule for a needed surgery, Lori leaned my direction and covered her mouth with her napkin. "I don't know about you," she whispered softly, "but I'd rather have the surgery." *I can't agree with you more,* I thought.

Regardless of how I feel about exercise and the excessive discussion thereof, it was difficult to argue with the results Linda and Mimi were getting. They were both stunning. *Didn't Scott deserve a thin, athletic, roaring wife too?* I sighed. "This chicken fat has to go!" I declared soon after that ladies' lunch date, and with courageous resolve, I took off running.

On "Day One" my son, Zeke, an athlete like his father, observed my warm-up time with refreshing candor, but I ignored his guffaws and skipped out the door. Somewhere around the bend of the first block, I thought I could hear the theme from *Chariots of Fire* playing in my head.

In little more than a week, I began running triathlons. Well, actually they were more like tri-ath-lawns. I would run past at least three lawns before collapsing. Then as I lay on the asphalt gasping for air, Scott would jog circles around me.

It was fun for awhile—both of us being athletes and all. But soon, I headed back to my books, finding it much more stimulating to read about exercise than to really do it.

Besides, I was thrilled to find that there are several practical and viable alternatives to losing weight. One method that works particularly well for me is diversion. This is how it goes: For the past thirty-nine years, I have been a brunette. Last week, however, I decided to try life as a semi-blond and had half of my hair glitzed in a golden hue. All week long, friends have been stopping me saying, "Something's different—have you lost weight?" See what I mean? For fifty bucks and two hours in a beauty shop, the world thought I'd lost ten pounds. The key is to do something so dramatically different to your head that you create a diversion from your well-padded body.

The second tactic has to do with the power of suggestion. I use this on my husband sometimes with amazing results. It works like this: I put on a dress in a size slightly larger than I normally wear and say, "Scott, would you look how much room there is in this dress?"

With no more prompting than that, he will usually comment, "I'm so proud of you, Honey. I could tell you were losing weight. Good job!" Or even though the scales may be shouting something to the contrary, I say aloud, "I'm feeling kind of thin today, sort of leaner and more energetic." With a knowing nod, Scott will affirm that he, too, has noticed how much I seem to be trimming up.

And finally, the easiest method of pseudo-weight control is camouflage. I recently bought a long dark plaid jumper, which fit well, with a nice wide belt, and paired it with a white, wide collared blouse. It was a size—hey, am I nuts? I'm not telling you that, but I will say it was in the upper teens. I immediately took it home, cut out the size tag and tossed that large number in the trash can. Who needs to know what size our clothes are anyway? If the dress *fits,* wear it! All I know is the fabric feels nice, and I feel pretty when I wear it. It's one of those outfits with long lines that makes everyone wonder if I've lost weight. I get all the psychological goodies without the stress of a diet— a win-win situation all around.

Now because I do want to stay somewhat fit, at least avoid coping with rigor mortis before I'm actually dead, I've invented my own "by-the-way" exercises. At stoplights, I take out a hand-held weight and pump some iron. (I call it auto-cize.) I also do isometrics for my hips and stomach while I type or drive, and knee bends and stretches while I brush my teeth. When the weather is pretty I'll take a walk and listen to a book on tape or just go to the grocery store and do aerobic shopping.

These are the things that work for me, that I can realistically incorporate into my day. A few minutes here and a few minutes there. Though I'll never be a tiny chick, my husband still crows when I'm by his side, my friends still cackle with joy when I waddle over to greet them, and my kids still nestle in this plump hen's arms for a hug at the end of a long day. When we boil down the chicken soup of life, aren't these the weighty matters that really count?

*Man looks at the outward appearance,
but the LORD looks at the heart.*
1 Samuel 16:7

Chicken Nugget

A 120-pound woman (for those of you who remember
what it was like to be one of those) can burn:

1. 3 calories per minute making the bed—more
   than bowling or walking at 2 miles per hour. (The
   downside of this is that there are only so many
   beds to make up in most houses, so you have to
   resort to unmaking and remaking them—if, that
   is, you want to burn more calories than are in an
   average ice cube.)
2. 3.5 calories per minute mopping—more than golf
   or riding horseback. (Although mopping WHILE
   riding horseback over a golf course really boosts
   the aerobic benefits.)
3. As many calories as she would burn backpacking,
   canoeing, skating, or chopping wood by dancing,
   weeding and digging around in the garden, or
   climbing stairs. (Oh, there's a cruel reminder. Not
   all of us GET to have stairs.)

Now if you'll excuse me, I must get to my digging
and dancing!

CHAPTER 5

Winging It through Wedded Bliss

by Gracie Malone

Before Joe and I got married, we thought we knew each other well. After all, we'd been friends almost three years and were well acquainted with each other's peculiarities and preferences. But almost as soon as we said, "I do," we started noticing things "we don't." For example, *we don't* usually agree on how to spend our free time.

I remember one Saturday morning in particular . . .

Anxious to begin a project—cleaning out the garage—I was up with the chickens, showered, and ready to go bright and early. With my "get it done" personality, I tend to think of weekends as the days God created to accommodate those things that can't be done during the Monday through Friday grind. Joe, on the other hand, with his laid-back disposition, believes the week's end should bring rest and relaxation. So while I was gearing up, visions of a well-organized, tidy garage dancing in my head, Joe was winding down by taking a long hot soak in the bathtub.

While Joe soaked away the morning, I stood in front of the sink, brushing my teeth with my right hand, polishing the marble with a towel in my left hand, closing the bottom drawer with my left foot, and memorizing a Scripture verse I'd taped on the mirror.

At one point, I glanced in Joe's direction. Three magazines, a mug of coffee, and his reading glasses were balanced precariously on top of the trash can near the tub. Warm steam fogged the glass doors, but I could see his reposed form, head cushioned on a plastic pillow stuck to the porcelain, and his yellow rubber ducky bobbing in the water. (When I bought it as a gag gift, I never dreamed he'd actually use it!) He was slowly plopping his big toe in and out of the water faucet—plop . . . drip . . . plop . . . drip—the soft rhythm transporting him into a state of euphoria.

How incredibly irritating!

With one hearty shove from my only remaining free limb—my right foot—I slammed the other drawer and waited, hoping for a response. Slowly and gently, Joe pushed the glass doors open just a crack, and looked at me as I continued to brush, swish, swipe, push, and memorize. "Gracie," he droned, "why don't you just relax?"

His words weren't profound, but they did cause me to stop and consider an important truth. At times I do need to slow my pace a bit. Why, I even have a hard time taking time out when I'm sick. On a few occasions, when I've been so weak I had to "recoop" in bed, I found myself restlessly thinking about all the things I'd rather be doing. Joe, on the other hand, seems to relish minor illnesses and sees them as an opportunity to stock up on TLC.

I discovered his preference one winter weekend . . .

Joe's throat had been so sore that he couldn't swallow, and his temperature checked in at 103 degrees. Doped up with antibiotics and painkillers, he was sleeping peacefully when I placed a glass of cool water on the night stand, turned out the light, tiptoed out of the room, and closed the door. *Now,* I thought, *my precious husband will enjoy the privilege of some much needed rest and relaxation.* Unfortunately, as soon as I closed the door, Joe woke up, and instead of feeling privileged, he felt abandoned. After a couple of hours in isolation, he came up with a clever plan.

I was reading in the living room when the phone rang. It was Judy, my friend who lived across the street. "Gracie," she chuckled, "Joe just called and asked me to relay a message. Would you please check on him? He needs some attention." For years now, Judy and I have laughed about Joe's pitiful SOS, and how a sore throat temporarily paralyzed his legs.

Over the years, Joe and I have learned to accept our inherent differences with good humor. But it hasn't always been easy. During the days when Matt and Mike were in grade school, mornings tended to be hectic. By the time the boys were dressed and ready to go, we finished breakfast, and Joe rummaged through the closet for clean clothes, I felt like I'd spent the morning chasing chickens in a large pen.

Of necessity, I mastered a few shortcuts. For example, I could pitch a clean white shirt into the clothes dryer, let it tumble for two minutes, remove it and shake out the wrinkles, touch it up with a hot iron, and send my hubby off to work looking as crisp and fresh as the next guy.

Joe was usually good-natured in the midst of the chaos. Usually! One morning I set three boxes of cereal on the table, plopped down a jug of milk, and sprinted to the utility room where the iron was heating on the ironing board. While pressing the collar of his shirt, I heard my husband's low grumble coming from the dining room. "Hot clothes and cold breakfast again today." Matt and Mike giggled as I darted back into the dining room, draped the shirt over Joe's shoulders, and paused to smooth his ruffled feathers.

Through many years of marriage, Joe and I eventually learned the art of compromise. He sends his shirts to the laundry, and I cook a hot breakfast on Saturdays. When I'm sick, he understands I prefer to be left alone and when he's cooped up, I know it's time for this hen to hover. More importantly, when it comes to handling our free time, Joe's speeded up some, and I've learned to enjoy more time out.

Once we planned a much-needed vacation—a week in the great Smoky Mountains. But much to our disappointment, it rained every day. By Saturday, we were running out of time, so I talked my husband into going shopping in lovely, historic Gatlinsburg—rain or no rain.

In the trunk of the car, I found an old dilapidated umbrella and we set out, arm in arm, determined to conquer the craft shops and the mini malls. We spent the next several hours darting between buildings, dodging puddles and downspouts, huddled bravely together beneath the single umbrella. Needless to say, we were soaked.

It was enough to make even an adventurous hen like me want to chicken out. I shrugged my shoulders and said, "I give up. I'm tired; I'm wet; let's go back to the motel."

Joe stopped on the sidewalk and studied me for a minute, carefully weighing the advantages of taking a nap in the cozy room, versus wasting the last day of a trip that had already cost him a wing and a leg. Finally he turned to me, rain dripping from his nose and eyeglasses, and with surprising pluck, declared, "Gracie, shut up and have fun!"

That line has become a classic and serves us well in our marriage. When we run into those inevitable differences, we can break the tension by reminding one another, "Hey, shut up and have fun!"

> *An excellent wife . . . smiles at the future. . . .*
> *She looks well to the ways of her household.*
> Proverbs 31:10, 25, 27 NASB

The "I Do's" and the "I Don'ts" of Marriage

Chicken Nugget

Do celebrate your differences. How boring "sameness" can be!

Don't try to change your mate.

Do respect each other. You are created in God's image.

Don't compromise your convictions. Every person is responsible for what they do.

Do pursue your God-given interests, talents, and spiritual gifts.

Don't expect your partner to meet all your needs. Needs are met in relationship with God.

Do develop a sense of humor. Learn to laugh at your mistakes.

Don't argue over irreconcilable differences. There are times when you must simply . . . *Shut up and have fun!*

CHAPTER 6

When a Rooster Comes Calling

by Rebecca Barlow Jordan

It was 12:10 A.M.—past my daughter's curfew—and I couldn't sleep. As I lay there awake, my anxious thoughts drifted back to the ups and downs of our girls' dating years. Early on, we had insisted on one important condition before "The Big Date": We would need to meet the prospective young man ahead of time. That, we hoped, would discourage any undesirables from the onset.

"I'm sorry. You'll have to ask my dad," worked to everyone's advantage. When our daughters didn't like the guys, they would clue Larry in ahead of time with, "Tell them *no,* Dad!" And we had the same right of refusal.

If a prospective date passed the first hurdle, the next step was an "instructional" encounter with Dad. Long before the first contestant arrived, we heard a variety of rumors through the "chickvine" concerning the requirements for roosters calling at the preacher's house. "If you want to date the preacher's daughter, you gotta memorize the book of John, recite the Lord's Prayer, and exegete the book of Revelation! And if her dad asks you where to find Joshua, *don't* tell him Joshua lives down the street."

"Sweet sixteen" at last, the magic day arrived for our youngest daughter, Jennifer. The first young man, a polite, guitar-picker destined for The Grand Ole Opry, passed the dating test, but they only dated once. We thought maybe it was because he crooned—or crowed—too loudly. The next two fellas never made it past the front door. Then came Rex, a suave, young "preacher boy." *How could we go wrong with someone in the ministry?* we reasoned. Larry carefully went over his five-point dating rules with Rex:

1. Do NOT pass GO. (Or I'll wring your rooster neck!)
2. Drive with BOTH hands on the wheel—and no flying allowed!
3. Keep in mind WHOSE you both are—The Lord's. (And what you'll be if you forget—a cooked goose!)
4. Our daughter IS a precious jewel, so treat her accordingly.
5. If you FAIL any one of rules one to four, I'll find you before the rooster crows three times!

I looked at the clock again, my humorous recollections evaporating like fog on a summer morning. Rex and Jen had been dating for some time now—long enough to earn a 12:00 curfew. But at 12:45 A.M., I woke Larry.

"Jen always calls if she's going to be late," I said. We had given them permission to go fishing but asked them to leave the area before dark. I assumed they would fish off the bank near the picnic site.

We called Rex's place of employment, in case they had stopped by there. Negative. Deep inside, we knew something was wrong. Larry paced, and I prayed. Then he prayed, and I paced. Tears begin to flow as I tried to erase the "What ifs?" Every time I closed my eyes to pray, I'd see floating bodies, boat wreckage, and missing person reports.

A few near tragedies drifted through my mind—the day our two-year-old Valerie drank gasoline, or the time we'd snatched her from the path of a speeding car on a busy California freeway. I remembered the day Jennifer sailed headfirst over her bicycle handlebars onto the street and the time she split her head on the door jam. Both girls endured feverish illnesses and several emergency trips to the hospital. But I'd never felt as fearful as I did right then. *Tragedy strikes other people,* I thought. *Why should I think we're any different?*

Half an hour later, Larry called Rex's parents. His dad said they had rented a fishing boat, and he knew where they were going. "Maybe we need to go out to the marina," he said to Larry with obvious concern.

A boat? I thought. *Rex never said anything about a boat! I sure hope he knows how to walk on water!* I resisted the urge to go with Larry and fulfill Dating Rule #5 myself. But I was more worried than angry at this point.

After Larry left, I woke our oldest daughter, Valerie; and together we talked, prayed, listened to praise music, and read aloud our familiar, family Scripture (Psalm 91) to bolster my own faltering confidence. My ruffled feathers smoothed out, and I began to feel God's calming assurance again.

At 2:30 A.M., Larry called and said they'd found Rex's car—but no sign of Rex or Jen. The storm inside of me began to rage again. They called the Sheriff Dispatch and tried to contact the engineer and owner of the marina. "The lake patrol is on its way," said Larry, trying to sound encouraging.

"Why don't they call the Coast Guard?" I asked. Valerie rolled her eyes. And then I realized we lived at least three hundred miles from any coast. At 3:30 A.M., I heard the phone ring again, and froze, realizing it could mean good news—or a tragedy. "Mom, answer it!" yelled Valerie.

It was Larry again. "They're safe." At the sound of Larry's reassuring voice, my heart rate subsided and every tense muscle relaxed—as if Jesus had spoken the same calming words to me that He had said to Peter on the Sea of Galilee that turbulent night: "Peace, be still!"

Details followed. Jen and Rex had pulled over to a small island for a picnic lunch. Just before dark, they tried to start the boat motor, but it stalled. For several hours they waited, hoping and watching for someone they could flag down. It was 3:00 A.M. before they heard a commotion nearby. A man had fallen asleep, and his sailboat had "accidentally" blown ashore on the island. The man, jarred awake as his boat hit the shore, offered to tow Rex and Jen's boat back to the marina.

About 4:30 A.M., Jen walked through the front door and into my arms. "I'm so sorry! I know you must have been worried!"

As I drifted to sleep in the wee hours of the morning, my earlier thoughts: *Would I see her again? Had I told her I loved her?* were replaced by the realization that my daughter was home again, safe at last. I nestled again gratefully in my faithful Father's arms, but not before adding a new family rule to the top of the list: No one leaves the house without a warm peck, an "I love you," and a hug around the neck!

You are precious and honored in my sight. . . . I love you.
Isaiah 43:4

Chicken Nugget

IF . . .
(with thanks to Rudyard Kipling)

If you can love your children
when they reject your faith;
If you can keep your hope
when all others turn away;
If you can praise your God
in the midst of adversity;
If you can believe the best,
when others cannot see;
If you can trust the Lord to
keep them safe from harm;
If you refuse the fearful
thoughts that only bring alarm;
If you can cling to Him,
no matter what may come.
You'll find your job of parenting
is a faithful job well done.

CHAPTER 7

Hen Hugs and Heart Tugs

by Fran Caffey Sandin

The phone rang as I measured ingredients for a batch of brownies. I grabbed the dishtowel, wiped my hands, and lifted the receiver. "Hello?"

"Hi, Fran. This is Brenda. The booster club needs another pan of chicken enchiladas for the concession stand tonight. Can you help us?" Before I could reply, the faint ding-dong of the doorbell sounded through the hallway.

"Brenda, can you hold? Someone's at my front door." Still wearing my apron, I ran to the front where I greeted Mr. Watson.

"Here are the brooms and cleaning supplies you ordered, Mrs. Sandin. Where would you like me to leave them?" Pointing to a corner in the entry, I apologized, excused myself, and raced back to the kitchen.

"Oh, sure, Brenda," I panted. "I'll work it in."

Cutting our conversation short, I trotted back to the front, paid Mr. Watson, and stashed my cleaning supplies in the closet. On my way back to the kitchen, I detoured to the utility room to place a load of clothes in the washer. *Wow, I'm really getting things done today!* I thought as I sorted the clothes into piles, loaded the machine, twirled the knob, and flew out of the utility room.

I raced back to the kitchen and stared at my brownie mix thoughtfully, *Did I or did I not add baking powder? Yes? No? Oh, I don't remember. I'll add a little more,* I reasoned. *Better to rise too much than to fall flat.*

After scooting the pan into the oven, I plucked a frozen chicken from the freezer, thawed it in the microwave, and began preparing the enchiladas. The aroma of home-baked chocolate brownies drifted through the house as I darted back and forth pitching clothes from the washer to the dryer.

As I popped open the dryer door to empty the final load, something strange fell out. *Where did that cute little baby sweater come from?* I wondered. The hot pink texture had a thick, spongy feel. Then it hit me. "Oh no! It can't be!" I squealed. "What on earth have I done?"

Angie at thirteen and supersensitive about her appearance, had one favorite sweater she treasured above all her other clothes. Each time she wore "the sweater" her friends showered her with compliments. Needless to say, Angie loved the attention and wore her prized possession at every opportunity.

Now the wool garment—never intended to see the inside of a washing machine—had shrunk to the size of one of her favorite stuffed animals—Snoopy—and it smelled like a real animal had been wearing it!

My knees felt weak and shaky and my heart raced as I considered my very limited options. I knew Angie would be crushed and angry. I just didn't know which would come first. While wondering if I should confess or let her find it for herself, I realized how hilarious it looked. I began smiling and then broke into fits of laughter. However, within my mother hen heart, I knew my little chick-a-dee would not be amused.

I took a deep breath when I heard Angie close the car door and bounce into the kitchen.

"Mom, what smells sooooooooo good? Wow! Those brownies are huge! May I have one?" she asked while reaching for a square. Her roller-coaster emotions in high gear, Angie nibbled on a brownie, and chatted about the big game and the party plans afterwards. Then she paused and assumed a dramatic flair.

"Mother," she said dreamily, her eyes glistening, "Doug may ask me to sit with him tonight and I want to wear my pink sweater—you know it's the best looking thing I own."

I'd heard about hot flashes. Now I had one. Picking up a magazine, I fanned my flushing face. "Angie," I began tremulously, "I'm afraid there's been a little accident." As I slipped into the utility room to retrieve the tragic remains, I braced myself for the explosion and prayed quietly under my breath, "Dear Lord, help us all."

Recognition triggered the first outburst. Angie grabbed the pot-holder sized garment from my hands, held it up, looked at me with a serious, horrified expression, and exclaimed, "No way!" After a short pause, her alto voice became high soprano as she squealed, "Mutheeeeeeerrrrrrrrrr! What did you do to my sweater?"

"I'm so sorry, Angie," I said softly, "I accidentally washed it with a load of towels. Wool sweaters have to be dry cleaned. Please forgive me. I promise to buy you a new sweater."

"Muuuthhheeeerrrrrr! How could you do this to me?" she howled. By this time we were both in tears. Trying to make the best of a bad situation, I decided to inject a note of humor. "Angie," I said cautiously, "I know it's not what you had in mind, but have you thought how cute Snoopy would look in that sweater?"

"MUTHERRRR!" she sobbed, "How could you even think such a thing at a time like this?"

"I'm so sorry, honey," I apologized. "Mothers are weird sometimes." With my place firmly secured in *The Guinness Book of Mama's Big Boo Boos*, I exited briskly before things got worse.

Later that afternoon, Angie recovered enough to find an alternative to "the sweater." She went to the game, the party, and Doug even asked her to sit with him. (Thank you, Jesus.) Within a few days, we were able to talk and laugh about the disaster. I replaced the original sweater with another pink one. (But I'll have to admit, it never had quite the pizzazz of the first.)

The sweater incident was only one of many times Angie and I clashed during her growing-up years, but we always found a way to mend our broken fences with forgiveness and lots of hugs. When Angie graduated from high school and left for college, a part of me departed, too. As I sat at home, sewing curtains for Angie's dorm room, I cried—not tears of sadness, not tears of happiness. Just a mother's heartfelt longing to hear her daughter's voice, to see her playing dolls, to watch her leading cheers, to feel her warm embrace.

Suddenly the collage of good times and bad times was framed by a special sweetness I could not appreciate while in the middle of the fray. The stormy times took on poignant significance as I thought, *Angie has taught me so much about living life with passion, and about learning patience and practicing unconditional love. (Even how to do the laundry!)*

Through the years, Angie and I have developed a close, loving, and very special relationship. We converse with ease and express ourselves openly and honestly. My little girl is married to a wonderful young man and has become the mother of Emily Grace, our first grandchild. As I recently watched Angie feeding her own baby daughter, I felt a strong heart tug, almost as though it was reaching across the generations of time.

As I cuddled Emily, stroked her velvet skin, and smelled her fresh baby powder fragrance, I thought, *Lord, thank you for a double blessing.* Then I lifted Emily's downy head next to mine and whispered in her ear, "Now wouldn't you look smashing in that little hot pink sweater? Too bad I didn't save it!"

He has made everything beautiful in its time.
Ecclesiastes 3:11

Chicken Nugget

Angie's Favorite Brownies

    1 cup sugar
    1 stick melted margarine
    2 eggs
    1 teaspoon vanilla
    ½ cup flour
    ½ teaspoon baking powder
    4 Tablespoons cocoa
    1 cup chopped walnuts or pecans

Mix ingredients; place in a well-greased 9-inch square pan. Bake at 350 degrees for exactly 35 minutes. Cut into small squares.

(For best results, do not double the baking powder!)

CHAPTER 8

The Roosters in Our Family Tree

by Gracie Malone

"May I kiss him?" our three-year-old grandson, Montana, asked as I started to place newborn Myles back in his cradle. I sat in the rocking chair, opened up the blanket, and watched as Montana kissed his little brother on the cheek. "Can I give him a hug?" he asked. When I nodded "yes," Montana put his arms around Myles' tiny shoulders and gently squeezed. "Let me tell him a secret." I cradled Myles in my arms while Montana leaned close to the baby's ear and whispered a secret message—something that no other person would ever know.

Throughout the day, at the most unexpected times, while watching *Toy Story* or playing with Mr. Potato Head™, Montana's thoughts would turn toward Myles and he'd jump up and ask, "May I kiss him? Give him a hug? Tell him a secret?" As I watched this tender scene unfold again and again, I thought about the special bond that exists between brothers—a bond that begins at birth, a bond so tight that even mothers and grandmothers are left wondering what the secret could possibly be.

As the mother of three sons, this wasn't the first time I'd seen the unique brotherhood that exists between guys born into the same family. Our oldest son, Matt, was two and a half when we brought his little brother, Mike, home from the hospital and gently laid him in the antique cradle that had rocked six generations of family members. One morning soon afterward, I heard a muffled voice coming from the baby's room. When I ran to check it out, there was Matt stretched out beside his brother, Mike's tiny fingers curled around Matt's slightly bigger ones. When I lifted him out of the cradle and explained why a big boy shouldn't climb into bed with such a tiny baby, Matt offered this simple excuse: "But, I wanted to tell him a story."

As they grew older, the bond between Matt and Mike grew stronger and secrets multiplied. I didn't find out the truth about some of their antics until after they were grown.

One summer we visited our friends in North Carolina— Gail, Virgil, and their three sons, Brian, Roger, and Daniel. On Friday night we put five little boys to bed early, and played bridge until the wee hours of the morning. Before we headed for the roost, I came up with a brilliant idea. "Let's put the cereal and the bowls on the table, and leave some milk in a small pitcher in the fridge. When the kids get up, they can eat breakfast and watch cartoons, while we sleep in."

The next morning when Gail stumbled into the kitchen and headed for the coffee pot, she found brightly colored cereal plastered all over the front of the refrigerator. Little trails of milk ran down the porcelain and dripped onto the floor. All experiments contain an element of risk, but this was appalling.

We finally learned that our precious sons had used their spoons as catapults, launching round after round of colorful ammunition at the white target. But to this day, it's still a mystery who came up with the idea or who did it first. With every question we asked, the ties that bind one brother to another grew tighter than the knots in their tennis shoe laces.

Throughout his grade school days and into the junior high years, Mike coveted Matt's "big brother" status with its privileges (and responsibilities). So about the time our number two son entered preadolescence, he started asking for a little brother. Needless to say, he received a somewhat-less-than-receptive response from me. So he went over my head and petitioned the one person he knew for certain would grant his wish—God. When I heard his prayers, I thought, I'd better feather my nest for a new baby chick.

Sure enough, Jason was born when Mike was twelve. That he was born on January first proved symbolic—new beginnings and a wide range of new experiences awaited us.

Before we brought him home from the hospital, my mother realized we needed help and decided to come for a visit. The first night, Jason was a toy. We played with him until bedtime, then slipped a cute little gown over his head, pulled the drawstring tight, placed him in the antique cradle, and settled down for a long winter's nap. At two o'clock in the morning, that cuddly little baby went off like a smoke alarm, and all five of us—Joe, Matt, Mike, Mother, and I—collided in the hallway, looking for the nearest exit.

From that night on, Jason's big brothers considered him their own personal charge. In addition to seeing that his basic needs were met, they made sure he enjoyed the coolest and best of life's experiences—a drop of lemon juice on his pacifier, a sip of pop, a taste of pizza, edited versions of "Monty Python." By the time he was three, Jason was a teen in a preschooler's body—more comfortable with a football than a stuffed toy, more in tune with "rock and roll" than lullabies, and most comfortable in a tiny pair of jeans and one of his kid-sized college T-shirts. He'd been biking, water skiing, camping, and motorcycling. He accompanied his brothers to football games, friend's houses, and the convenience store parking lot. (Matt finally confessed that Jason attracted girls like a magnet. "Why, he gets more attention than my Irish setter!")

At home, Jason would likely be clutching a tattered and faded blue blanket as he perched on Mike's back to watch TV or sat on the hood of Matt's sports car cheering the teens shooting hoops in our driveway. And he was always giggling over something whispered into his ear.

By the time Matt and Mike went away to college, they were confident that Jason was thoroughly prepared for kindergarten—after all, they had already taught him several of the basic laws of science and physics. I came home from the grocery store one day and found Matt holding Jason upside down over the banister on the second floor level. Mike stood on the first floor with his arms extended to catch him in case Matt's hands slipped. "We're just teaching him about the laws of gravity," they explained as I fussed and sputtered. They taught him about aerodynamics by sending him running as fast as he could go through the living room dodging flying pillows. They taught him physics by spinning him around and around in circles, then watching him fall in a crumpled heap. They helped him discover the beauty of God's creation by having him look up toward heaven until his face was covered with light, fluffy snowflakes.

When Matt and Mike went away to school, Jason did quite well on his own, developing into a sensitive, strong, intelligent guy, with lots of close friends. And he kept in touch with his brothers regularly by phone. When Jason finished college, I wasn't surprised that Matt offered him a job. "Come to work for us, and I'll teach you all I know about how to run a business."

It seems to me that the sentiment Montana expressed toward Myles is still being passed down from brother to brother. Oh, I know they would gag to think about puckering up for a kiss, but I have seen them exchange a few awkward hugs. And they are still sharing secrets.

> *How good and pleasant it is when*
> *brothers live together in unity!*
> Psalm 133:1

Chicken Nugget

From
What Is a Boy . . .
(Author Unknown)

A boy is Truth with dirt on its face,
Beauty with a cut on its finger,
Wisdom with bubble gum in its hair,
and the Hope of the future
with a frog in its pocket.

CHAPTER 9

In the Throes of Mother Henhood

by Becky Freeman

It was the perfect night for high school football—a beautiful October evening in Texas. The air was crisp, the band was playing something patriotic and snappy, and the Buffalos' red uniforms, contrasted with the blue shirts worn by the other team, looked so lovely against the green field. (We women notice those things.)

All was bright and beautiful until our son Zeke, a junior, went down on the football field and didn't get back up—every parent's nightmare.

As the paramedics rushed forward, my husband, Scott, took the bleacher steps two at a time, bounded over the tall fence, and rushed to our son. I ran along behind him, my heart in my throat. Then I came face to face with the fence. *What to do, what to do?* I stopped for a fleeting second and thought, *If I climb this fence and Zeke is okay, he will be embarrassed for the rest of his mortal life. If I don't, I will have to fight every mother hen instinct in my body, all of which are screaming for me to get to my hurting child.*

What can I say? I'm a Mom—I climbed.

When I got to the sidelines, Scott looked up and caught my eye, motioning for me to return to "the mother spot"—on the other side of the fence. "Dislocated elbow," he yelled. "Go get the car and meet us at the hospital with the insurance forms."

I retraced my steps, my legs feeling as though they belonged to a rubber chicken, then once again, I came to the fence. In the moments since I had valiantly tackled it—it had *grown!*

Try as I might, I could not get over the thing, so the cheerleaders gathered around me in pyramid formation and shoved me up and over, where I landed in a heap and injured my own knee. A kind man and good friend helped me off the field and drove me to the hospital. (He also discreetly pointed out that there was a gate not five yards from where I'd taken my undignified tumble.)

My knee was terribly sprained, but I felt nothing until the next day—nothing hurt that night but my heart. Hobbling into the emergency room to see my son, I couldn't help noticing how beautiful and filthy he was, part little boy and part grown man.

"Mom?" he asked as he lay there with his arm outstretched and wrapped in splints, his eyes filled with pain—"why are *you* limping?"

I hopped on one leg until I was near enough to put my arms around him. "I'm fine," I said, "it's just a mother hen thing." He looked confused but I didn't explain as I leaned on the clean white pillow, stroking and kissing his cheek. "And how are you, son?"

"I'll be okay, Mom," he said, his voice breaking only slightly, "God was with me."

I forget that sometimes. But what a comforting thought. I can't always be with my children. I can't always protect them, though the Lord knows how much I want to. The good news is that God's presence knows no bounds. He can be father, mother, friend, and brother to our kids—at least until we moms can waddle in and give them a kiss on the cheek.

The aftermath of Zeke's injury brought with it a torrent of questions, followed by agonizing decisions. He so wanted to play again. "Mom," he implored, "I always finish what I start. I can't let my team and my coaches down!" But like all parents who climb up endless bleachers in the rain, cold, and dark of night to cheer their child, Scott and I worried that some moment of glory might leave Zeke with long-lasting health problems.

I was convinced the pain was no longer worth the gain. With conviction I told him, "Son, there's more to life than football." He nodded sadly, and walked out the door to school.

Then one afternoon I drove to the high school to pick up my daughter and saw Zeke running around the track with all his might, his swollen arm in a splint. He must have been in some pain but his eyes were set on the track ahead of him, with the exception of an occasional glance at his teammates who were practicing in the field next to him. I could see Zeke was determined to stay in the best possible condition, just in case the doctors gave him the go-ahead, and he could convince his parents to let him play the remaining games of the season.

For the several Friday nights following, Scott and I observed Zeke standing on the sideline as he cheered his team on. Every tensed sinew of his muscular frame, every intense facial expression revealed his heartache, his longing to be out on the field making tackles and blocking field goals in this crazy game—the classic American "clanhood of manhood."

As a mother, I confess I don't understand the instinctual draw between men and sports, but I've begun to accept that most men are born with a need to fight hard and win. Trying to stop them is like trying to stop the wind or a great tidal wave of testosterone. And so, when the doctor agreed that Zeke could play the last three games of the season (most likely the last three "real" football games of his life), how could we say "no"?

"Yes" was a desperately difficult path, however. I felt the courage drain from my body every time Zeke went out on the field. The best I could do was to close my eyes and pray until the play was safely over. As expected, Zeke played with all his might, as did his teammates, launching the Lone Oak Buffalos into the regional playoffs. Best of all, to this mother's relief, Zeke survived the season unscathed by any further injuries.

Last week Scott and I went to the Lone Oak high school sports banquet. The walls were covered with poster-sized photos of the boys during the past season. There was a photo of Zeke running through a paper sign as he charged onto the field, another showed him dressed as a cheerleader at a pep rally, and one more pictured him locked in an after-game huddle of victory with his coaches and teammates.

But my eye kept returning to a photo of Zeke with his arm in a splint standing on the sidelines—a wistful look in his eyes. *Let me out there,* he seemed to be thinking. *Please, Lord, give me a chance to get out there and play again!*

After our meal and toward the close of the awards ceremony, Coach Turner stood at the podium and said, "There is only one award each year given by the coach to a player who has shown great heart, will, desire, and effort while over-coming obstacles. The award isn't always given to the most talented player, although this young man is loaded with talent." At that point, the coach chuckled and added, "Now this kid marches to the beat of a different drummer sometimes, but no one at this school can deny that he puts his whole heart into everything he does. He is a great Christian kid, whose faith has been put to the test time and time again. This year's Jack Brookins Fighting Heart Award goes to—Zeke Freeman."

What can I say? I'm a mom. I cried.

Let your eyes look straight ahead,
fix your gaze directly before you.
Proverbs 4:25
(Zeke's favorite Bible verse, pinned to his wall)

Chicken Nugget

To James

by Frank Horne

(from Zeke's favorite poem)

From *Prentice Hall Literature Book,*
Prentice Hall, A Division of Simon & Schuster
Englewood Cliffs, New Jersey 07632

Live
as I have taught you
to run, Boy—
it's a short dash.
Dig your starting holes
deep and firm
lurch out of them
into the straightway
with all the power
that is in you
look straight ahead
to the finish line
think only of the goal
run straight
run high
run hard
save nothing
and finish
with an ecstatic burst
that carries you
hurtling
through the tape
to the victory. . . .

SECTION II

Just among Hens

Courage in Nurturing Friendships

CHAPTER 10

Flying with the Eagles

by Rebecca Barlow Jordan

When we started working with senior adults at our church, I thought, *That shouldn't take too much energy. After all, most seniors are retired.* However, I soon learned that *retired* did not mean tired. These "keenagers," who call themselves "young at heart," managed to reverse every myth we'd ever heard about seniors: They don't all reside in nursing homes. They aren't all alone and lonely. And a great many of them are certainly not living in poverty.

If you arrive fifteen minutes early before leaving on a trip, they ask, "What kept you?" They've warmed their van seats at least an hour ahead of departure. On our longer road trips, we no sooner bed down for the night than the smell of morning coffee reaches my nose. Our fellow travelers rise up before the rooster crows, and they are pacing the lobby, ready to go.

On one of our recent trips to Ridgecrest, North Carolina, we squeezed in a side trip to a nearby tourist attraction: Chimney Rock. After riding up the mountainside on an elevator, some of the heartier seniors climbed from lookout point up to the top—about eighty-four stairs. I was snapping pictures and enjoying the breathtaking view when I looked back down the steps. There, one of our gentlemen in his eighties, cane in hand, was steadily tap-tapping his way up the steep incline.

"Lonnie, what on earth are you doing?" I yelled, running down to try and head him off. One of our seniors had fallen earlier in the day, and I didn't want another one hurt.

"I wanted a picture of me on top of this mountain," he grinned mischievously. I grabbed his arm and escorted him the rest of the way up—and then back down again.

As he wobbled back down the hill, he reminded me of Caleb, an eighty-five-year-old Bible character, who shouted, "Give me this mountain!" and with God's help, conquered every remaining enemy—including fear—as he "climbed" to the peak.

I needn't worry about our folks. On some trips, even after night services, many still have the energy to pull out the card tables for a few games of "Chickenfoot"—and some vanilla ice cream.

On a journey to Eureka Springs, Arkansas, we attended the *Passion Play*. Great seats with one little problem—they were about a hundred steps downhill. Afterwards, we heaved and hoed our way back to the top. Once there, we located a wheel-chair for one of our senior ladies who complained of weak knees and lightheadedness. But by the time a first aid attendant took her pulse, it was normal: 72. On the other hand, I estimated my own at about 100. I was still huffing and puffing long after some of them were asleep for the night.

On a small-scale "Holy Land" tour that same day, we met a woman regaled in biblical garb and walking about in a cool, dark cave. She introduced herself as the character "Martha," a keeper of the cave where Jesus was born. She and her retired husband had moved to Eureka Springs, she told us, with nothing but an availability and willingness to serve God. Her voice increased a few decibels with each sentence as she narrated the familiar script. "Scores of visitors come here each day to hear the story of Jesus. Just think! This same Jesus—God's own Son—is coming back again for all of us!"

You could have heard a pebble drop in the eerie silence as her final words echoed through the cave. Before I knew what was happening, I opened my mouth and shouted, "Hallelujah!"

A crimson blush crept up my face as a dozen pair of our seniors' eyes—and Martha's—stared at me in unison. "Honey," Martha's syrupy voice startled me, "would you lead us in a stanza of 'Amazing Grace'?" So I did. As we stood hand in hand, reluctant to leave, salty tears trickled down our faces.

In addition to her daytime portrayal of Martha, this precious woman also acted every night in the *Passion Play.* Her husband, perched steadily on two leg braces, reenacted the Lord's Supper for us in another nearby cave. I left that hallowed place strangely warmed, rethinking the meaning of "retirement."

Some of our longer trips often trigger a few physical ailments—but not for long. The jokes roll out in perfect rhythm with the tires of the long white vans—and laughter soon dispels any hint of discomfort. Some of them, like Thurman and Neel, come armed with a fresh supply of humorous stories, gathered from years of experience. Neel recently told one of my favorites:

One day as Neel returned home from the drugstore, he noticed a car had followed him right into his own driveway. He got out, and there sat an unoccupied Volkswagen joined to his car, chrome to chrome, like a Siamese twin. He had accidentally backed into it getting out of a tight parking place. He called the store and told them what had happened. Herbert, the store owner, started laughing. "Neel, the man has already reported his car stolen." Within a few minutes, Herbert and the other man arrived at Neel's house to unhook the bumpers and pick up the Volkswagen™.

Another time Neel was trying to impress his brother-in-law with his new 1928 Chevrolet™ sedan. To demonstrate the superior braking system, he stopped suddenly. Both doors popped off and slid across the brick pavement by the courthouse, along with a few bolts, and Neel's pride, no doubt.

A few years back, I attended a women's retreat in the hills of Oklahoma with several women from our church. New conference attendees were asked to take certain basic, required classes, so Imogene and I found our seats and focused in on the speaker. A few minutes later, I looked over at this tiny, eighty-year-old grandmother who could have taught us all—one whom I affectionately call "Giggles." There she was, snickering into her cupped hands and thoroughly enjoying the speaker's humor. The subject? "The Joy of Sex in Marriage."

Our seniors tote their paintbrushes, their chicken casseroles and cookies, their warm smiles and helping hands to the homebound, nursing homes, hospitals, apartments, and church classrooms. They read aloud *The Good Samaritan* in vacation Bible school or *The Velveteen Rabbit* in public school, demonstrating real love to a bunch of wiggly preschoolers. And at any hour of the day, you may find one of our senior "prayer warriors" lifting up names and needs before the Heavenly Father.

It could be their faithful preparation that keeps our seniors flying. Before every trip, they remind each other: "Do you have your bifocals? Bran? Ben-Gay? Bufferin? Pills? Heating pad and Polygrip?" Or maybe they fuel their energy with the extra calories they sock away at those eat-all-you-want buffets.

Nancy, one of the leaders who fusses over our seniors like a mother hen, says, "We try to prepare for the unexpected, but it is the Lord Who always prepares us, no matter what happens. His angels are there, constantly guarding and providing."

There's never a dull moment with our senior friends. Whether it's pulling each other in a Red Flyer™ wagon through The Antique Rose Emporium, tiptoeing through the golden daffodils at Gladewater, or standing on holy ground inside the Cove, Billy Graham's training center in North Carolina—you need your running shoes to keep up with them.

As for me, I find it hard to be a chicken when I'm soaring with these eagles.

Praise the Lord . . . who satisfies your desires with good things so that your youth is renewed like the eagle's.
Psalm 103:2,5

Youthful Secrets from the Eagles' Nest
Taken from My Grandmother's Scrapbook

Chicken Nugget

1. **For strained eyes or headache,** cut off each end of a raw cucumber and place a piece over each eye. Relax while the cucumber draws out pain and fatigue.

2. **For aching feet, corns, or bunions,** make a poultice of chopped garlic. Apply this to sore spot and leave on for several hours to relieve inflammation. (If it doesn't get rid of the pain, at least it should drive away your enemies.)

3. **For soft hair and skin,** gather up morning dew from shrubs and grass with the palm of your hand. Pat it on your face. Save rainwater to use when washing your hair.

CHAPTER 11

A Ruckus in the Henhouse

by Gracie Malone

When the doorbell rang one evening at 9:30 P.M., I switched off the TV and pretended to be sleeping, but my husband, Joe, invited Becky in. She marched down the hall into the bedroom, plopped on my bed, and folded her drumsticks beneath her. As she clutched a feather pillow tightly in her arms, I thought, *This chick is planning to nest here until our problem is solved.*

I had nothing left to say. E-mail messages had been flying back and forth in the cyberspace between Becky's house and mine all afternoon. "I've just got one thing to say . . ."

"Dear, one thing . . .

"One more thing, and I'm done . . ."

"Dear, almost done . . ."

"I'm done . . ."

"Dear, done . . ."

By the time we got to "done," I was not only "done," I was "done in." I literally cried all afternoon, my eyes burning and my nose so tender I couldn't touch it with a tissue. I was, as we say here in Chickendom, mad as an old wet hen.

Earlier in the day, as Becky and I were sipping coffee with friends, a misunderstanding arose in the group. I decided to confront the issue head on by "speaking the truth in love." Unfortunately, the confrontation was dreadfully out of balance— heavy on "truth," light on love.

When I sent my first message to Becky, I simply wanted to clarify my point of view. *How could she not agree with me?* After all, I consider her one of my closest friends, a true kindred spirit. But alas, after one round of verbal "tug of war," the situation became obvious. Becky disagreed with me! And I couldn't change her mind during round two, or even round three. Finally, I gave up trying to convince her I was right, and wondered, *Is it possible that I, the most mature—or at least the most "chronologically gifted"—member of the group could actually be wrong?*

I felt depressed and hurt. I felt positively unappreciated. I put on my ugliest pajamas and crawled into bed early. Then Becky came over and perched on the roost next to me, determined to talk, even though I was all talked out. I honestly wanted to hit her with the other pillow, but I didn't have the energy to hoist the king-sized projectile above my head. Besides that, I knew I couldn't deck my friend with a bag of feathers. My heart softened as soon as she choked out the words, "What have I done to you?"

In the dim light reflecting from the hallway, I could see Becky's little girl face—her eyes downcast, and one perfectly manicured fingernail pecking a staccato rhythm on her pearly white front tooth. I was overcome with the strangest mixture of emotion—love, frustration, anger, and, as always when the two of us get together, humor. I blurted out exactly what I thought. "Becky Freeman, you are the meanest friend in the whole wide world."

I would have said more, but my dog, my own faithful, loyal, dachshund, Porsche, jumped on the bed with a tennis ball in her mouth and started wagging her tail and licking Becky's hand as if we had gathered to play ball.

"Porsche, stop wagging your tail," I blubbered, "we are not having fun!" With this pronouncement, Becky and I burst out laughing, and for the next hour, we talked and cried and laughed.

My strained relationship with Becky hurt deeply. I knew we had to talk—really communicate, not just fire off verbal ammunition from minds already made up. But here in my bedroom, with our fragile feelings exposed and raw, it was harder to "speak the truth"—much easier simply to love.

"Becky," I began, "how could you imply that I would purposely hurt someone?"

"That's not what I meant to say," she cajoled.

"Well, when I spoke up in the group, did I sound like a mean old woman?" I asked, my eyes pleading.

"No, you didn't sound like a mean old woman, just kind of middle-aged mean," Becky answered. As the discussion continued, the issues became much less emotional, more rational, and I might add, a lot less funny.

"Becky," I explained, "love has to be based on truth or it isn't love at all. Sometimes, in order for truth to prevail, our feelings get hurt in the process. Love needs to be tough. It would have been easier to ignore the issues, sweep our problems under the carpet, tap it down, and let it lie. Our meeting would have been much nicer, and I would have come home feeling better, but we would have missed an opportunity to grow. You may not believe it, but my actions today were motivated by love."

"But, Gracie," Becky came back, "what you said didn't sound like truth wrapped in love. Love should be tender. A person's got to feel accepted, have permission to fail; then there is freedom to open up about faults without fear of rejection. God requires us to 'walk justly and love mercy.' To me, that means we are supposed to be just, but we're also expected to be consumed with a passion for showing mercy. When it comes to justice or mercy, I lean toward mercy."

Eventually we realized that the problems between us had more to do with our unique ways of seeing things, our spiritual gifts, and our differing techniques for handling conflict than the rightness or wrongness of our thinking. Actually, both of us were right in some ways, and wrong in others.

I reached for Becky's hand and we prayed together. Then Becky said, "Please don't stop loving me and being my friend just because we are different in the way we view things."

Later, I thought about how fragile this thing called friendship really is, and how close Becky and I had come to losing something precious. In our group, we've laughed and cried, expressed our grief, exposed our pain, and occasionally resisted the urge to pluck out each other's feathers. But our love for each other has never diminished. Our friendship, with all its ups and downs, rests upon the rock solid, never changing, always sustaining, love of God.

Do I love my circle of friends? Of course I do. Will I ever stop being friends with Becky? Never! Why, I love her more than my wee dog!

Faithful are the wounds of a friend.
Proverbs 27:6 KJV

Chicken Nugget

"Always
it is more important
that we retain
a right spirit toward others
than that we bring them to
our way of thinking,
even if our way is right."

A. W. Tozer

Oh, the comfort—the inexpressible
Comfort of feeling safe with a person,
Having neither to weigh thoughts,
Nor measure words—but pouring them
All right out—just as they are—
Chaff and grain together—
Certain that a faithful hand will
Take and sift them—
Keep what is worth keeping—
And with the breath of kindness
Blow the rest away.

Dinah Marie Mulock Craik

CHAPTER 12

Tearin' Down the Fence

by Rebecca Barlow Jordan

My clammy hands and racing pulse threatened to reveal the terror hiding inside my chicken heart. *Will he make it? What will Mom do if she loses him? God, please don't take my daddy yet.*

Two previous heart attacks had necessitated my father's early retirement. Now a routine cauterization revealed the unexpected need for triple bypass surgery. The operation lasted more than five hours, but for Mom and me, the waiting continued. At one point, a nurse told us the surgery was over, and we could see Daddy upstairs in a few minutes. But an hour later, we finally stopped another nurse passing by.

"Oh, didn't anyone tell you?" she looked puzzled. "Your father's back in surgery. Something about complications and bleeding." Mother fell into my arms, crying uncontrollably.

"It will be all right," I said to her repeatedly. *And it will be,* I seemed to hear God whisper.

At that moment, I felt God's own reassuring arms surrounding the two of us. I remembered truths my husband and father (both pastors) had taught: In adversity, God develops special qualities of love and sensitivity in our hearts. That process of waiting, through moments of anxiety, prepares us to comfort others, because often our most effective counsel grows out of our own difficulties.

My first opportunity to utter those comforting words, "I know what you're going through," came while waiting with family members of other heart patients. Within forty-eight hours, five out of eight families in that circle of suffering had lost their loved ones. My mom and I exchanged silent, sympathetic hugs and tears with those gathered there.

During my father's surgery, a young Hispanic girl named Fidlina approached me. "Hablo espanol?" she asked. (Do you speak Spanish?) "Muy poquito!" I replied, with a strong emphasis on the muy (very little). Spanish words slid off her tongue faster than an egg rolls downhill. I held out my hand like a traffic cop. "Stop! Slow down!"

Through her broken English and hand motions, I determined she was trying to find out the condition of her baby daughter, who was also in surgery. I must have sounded like a purring cat every time I trilled the r's of my English words: "Fidlina, I'll be prrrrraying for your baby."

Desperate to communicate, I reverted to sign language— as if she were deaf, rather than Hispanic. Finally, I took Fidlina over to the hospital information desk. "Is there anyone here who can tell this lady about her baby?" I asked. Several minutes later, a petite, Hispanic nurse rounded the corner. I watched them talk fluently, and Fidlina soon returned. "Muchas gracias! Muchas gracias!" she thanked me.

She still looked lonely and fearful, so I sat down beside the young mother again. Why hadn't I taken Spanish in high school or college? I tried out all the words I thought I knew: *"Mama, Papa, taco y enchilada, sí, adios."* But conversation soon came to a dead end. I felt as though an invisible fence—

or wall—stood between the two of us. How could I break through and convey God's comfort and strength? "I need help, God," I whispered.

I left Fidlina and walked down the hallway of the busy hospital until I located a small chapel. The door stood open, and inside the walls of that empty cathedral, it seemed an invisible sign hung across its hallowed stained-glass windows: "Heavy hearts welcome." Nestling in a quiet corner and preparing to enter Heaven's presence, I smiled as I remembered my own feeble attempts to communicate on a mission trip to Mexico a few years earlier.

In my zeal to impress the locals with my Spanish vocabulary, I said repeatedly, *"La comoda, la comoda."* Finally one sweet Hispanic woman took me aside and explained that I was asking for a chest of drawers. *La comoda* sounded like "bathroom" to me.

I took a deep breath, then plunged in, praying, "Lord, the words I need are scrambled inside my brain, and I've already botched three attempts to use last year's 'Spanish-in-Three-Easy-Lessons.' Would You please help me talk with Fidlina?" I pleaded.

As I returned to my new *"amiga,"* familiar words and phrases, learned as a child in a bilingual school of Weslaco, Texas, flew through my mind. I half ran to Fidlina's side, speaking earnestly and eagerly, "When *Jesus Christos* came into *mi corazon,* (my heart) He changed my life." I told her how He had become my best friend, and that He could be her "amigo," too.

Her dark eyes lit up as she knowingly pointed toward Heaven and then to her heart in agreement. *"Sí, Sí!"* During that week, Fidlina called me her *"poquita Espanol amiga,"* (her little Spanish friend). Each day I checked on the young mother and her baby, and each day Fidlina asked about my *"papa"* as well.

One day we walked together through the long corridors of the massive hospital, and I stood beside Fidlina, rejoicing with her. Tears filled my eyes as she smiled and gestured to her tiny infant, now recuperating nicely in the hospital nursery.

When I left the hospital, Fidlina and I embraced. She extended an invitation for me to visit her and eat "frijoles and tortillas," and I asked her to come over for chicken and dressing. In one week, God ripped away the fence that had separated us from each other. In God's coop, there are no barriers too great to crash through. With family, friends, or strangers, His love will always find a way—even if that means enrolling in a Spanish refresher course. Yes, ol' chicks can learn new tricks.

With my God I can scale a wall.
Psalm 18:29

Rebecca's Mexican Chicken Soup

Chicken Nugget

2 cans Campbell's Southwest
  Chicken Vegetable Soup™
2 cans water
½ onion, chopped
1-2 carrots, sliced thinly
Leftover veggies in the refrigerator (optional)
½ -1 can green beans
1 cup cooked Fajita chicken strips (or small chunks
  of cooked chicken)

Mix above ingredients in large saucepan. Then sprinkle in the following to taste: garlic salt, Italian seasoning, dried Basil, several drops of Louisiana Hot Sauce™, and dried parsley flakes. Add additional water if necessary. (A chicken bouillon cube will keep the chicken flavor strong.) Let simmer for 10-15 minutes or until fresh vegetables are tender. Just before ready to serve, stir 1-2 ounces of Velvetta™ cheese into soup until melted.

Serve with Mexican cornbread.
Makes four generous servings.
(Double recipe for a crowd.)

CHAPTER 13

Chicken to Go

by Gracie Malone

I think I've figured out the answer to the question, "Why did the chicken cross the road?" She wanted to go to town—to shop, to do lunch with friends, to run errands. And she was determined to overcome any obstacle to do so, including making a mad dash across the highway. When a chicken's got her heart set on going somewhere, neither rain nor sleet nor dark of night can keep her from her appointed rounds.

I experienced such an urge one morning a few years back. It had been raining for one full week, and I had been cooped up for three days. The Sabine River had overflowed its banks, flooding the creek that ran along the boundary of our property and creating a lake in our low-lying pasture. Of the two roads leading from our house into town, one was obviously impassable, with water at least eighteen inches deep covering the iron bridge that spanned the creek. The other road was questionable. I decided that questionable was worth a shot.

My little car roared down the farm-to-market road till I came to a low place where the blacktop was completely under water. I gauged the water to be about eight or ten inches deep by checking the fence posts and barbed wire on both sides of the road. *Hmmm, seems about ten or twelve inches from the bottom of my car to the surface of the road,* I speculated. With a quick mental calculation, I estimated that there could be as much as four inches to spare.

For just a moment, I considered playing it safe and going back home, but then I remembered how isolated and bored I'd been. *I'm goin' for it,* I declared, taking a deep breath and floorboarding it. Water rolled up the sides of my car in waves that would have made Charleton Heston proud. But just as I was about to shout, "I'm free at last!" my car chugged, sputtered, and stopped. Water poured in one door and out the other as I grabbed my purse, climbed free, and waded to higher ground.

When I reached dry land, I stopped to pour water out of my shoes and noticed a farmer heading my direction on a tractor. He shook his head as he pulled into the water and hooked a chain on my bumper. "What were you thinking, Ma'am," he sighed. "You 'spect them waters to part like the Red Sea?"

I shrugged my shoulders and thought, *Yep, guess I did.* That evening my husband towed the car home, vacuumed it out, and got it running again. When he pulled the spark plugs, water dripped off the points and ran out of the little holes they were plugged into. It's a wonder, but that car continued to serve me well for several more years, providing a dependable way for this "chicken to go." But I never wheeled my way through high water again.

I'm not the only chick who's had trouble trying to cross the road. My friend Judy was on her way to the mall when she realized something was wrong with her car. She stopped by the office and explained her situation to several coworkers, who in turn put their heads together—under the hood of her new Buick™—and diagnosed the problem.

"See this cable?" one fellow asked. "It's frayed, not making good contact. You should drive to the dealer and get it replaced."

Judy climbed back into the driver's seat and headed toward the dealership where she had recently purchased her car. On the way, she whipped out her cell phone and called Jerry, her beloved husband. "Hon," she chirped, "my car's acting up. Would you meet me at the garage and talk to the mechanic?" Jerry, a retired gentleman with a laid-back disposition, pulled on his khakis and T-shirt, slipped his feet into a pair of comfy loafers, and dutifully set out to meet his wife.

In the thirty-something years I've known Judy and Jerry, I've never ceased to be amazed at how their relationship proves the adage that "opposites attract." Jerry, a slow-moving, deep-thinking, solid-rock kind of guy is teamed up with Judy, a fast-paced, emotionally charged woman who can't seem to keep her hormones in balance. In the drama that unfolded, their contrasting personalities played a major role.

As Judy steamrolled toward her destination, Jerry strolled out to his truck and motored toward the appointed place, being sure to stay well within the speed limits. Meanwhile, Judy got stuck in traffic. *Oh no*, she thought, *what if the car dies and I can't get it started again?* The idea had scarcely passed through her mind when, like a self-fulfilling prophecy, the car sputtered, chugged, and gave up the ghost.

Judy said, "After that, I learned firsthand how impolite people can be when a fellow motorist has car trouble. The driver of the pickup behind me blasted his horn. Everybody else zipped around me, flailing their arms and pointing upward in a most exasperated manner."

To avoid becoming the city's latest victim of road rage, Judy decided to get out of the car and raise the hood—the standard sign of a driver in distress. But when she tried to open the door, the automatic locks held fast. She pressed the button to lower the window, but her power windows were sealed tighter than the lid on a pressure cooker. She pounded the horn, but it didn't work. She reached for her cell phone. Since it depended on the car's battery for its power, it wouldn't work either.

By this time Judy was beginning to bake. In the sizzling month of July, Texas temperatures inside a closed car can quickly soar to oven-like proportions. *I'll break the window,* Judy decided. She searched for a pair of pliers, a screwdriver— anything that could break glass, but she couldn't find a single hard object. So, irrational though it may be, she decided to break the window with her bare hands. She pounded frantically until a man driving a Sears truck pulled up beside her, glanced her way, and mouthed the words, "It's okay."

In a flash, the Good Samaritan pulled in front of Judy's car, and jumped out with battery cables in hand. Judy popped the hood with the manual lever. While the man worked steadily on the engine, the scene unfolding inside the car took on the flavor of an "I Love Lucy" episode. Spotting a cup half full of soft drink in the drink holder, Judy scooped up a handful of crushed ice and the syrupy liquid and started rubbing it on her face and arms. Before long, she felt like a roasted chicken marinated in molasses. And then she saw Jerry.

"He pulled onto the nearby mall parking lot, slid out of his truck, and slowly sauntered toward us as only Jerry can," Judy said. "With his hands shoved in his pockets, kicking gravel, I could tell he was thinking, *Car trouble again!*"

Then Jerry committed a grievous error in judgment (albeit a typical male response). Instead of checking on Judy first, he stuck his head under the hood of the car. At that point, Judy's emotions took a sudden U-turn. No longer terrified, now sheer fury drove her into action. She socked her hand into the cup, grabbed a handful of ice, and threw it at him. Of course it splattered on the windshield and bounced back in her lap. "Get me out of this car!" she bellowed.

Fortunately, the guys had just come up with a plan. Jerry yelled, "Put one hand on the door handle, the other on the ignition key. When I say go, try to start the car. Maybe you'll have one second of power when you can open the door." They held the frayed ends of the wire together and yelled, "Go!" While the cable arced, Judy turned the key, and opened the door.

She flounced out of the car, trudged across the parking lot, perched in the seat of Jerry's truck, and turned the air-conditioning vents full in her face. As the cool air from the truck's air conditioner soothed her ruffled feathers, Judy took a good look at herself. Her arms were finger-painted with a mixture of cola and sweat, a lock of hair plastered to her forehead dangled over one eye, and her dress sported a new pattern of sticky brown spots. She had to laugh—her usual sense of humor returning just in time to relieve the tension.

Soon the car was towed to the shop, and Judy stood by Jerry's side as he explained the problem to the mechanic. He listened then glanced Judy's way and said, "Ma'am, I need to show you something." Escorting Judy and Jerry to the driver's side of the immobilized car, he opened the door, and pointed to a tiny lever underneath the door handle. "This is the emergency handle." He flipped the tiny lever back and forth while the door latch popped in and out. Later Judy admitted, "I felt like such a dumb cluck. The whole drama could have been avoided if only I had known. . . ."

"If only I had known" has been the cry of many a stranded hen as she ventured out onto life's perilous roads. We can do our best to avoid danger, to prepare for emergencies, but our trust ultimately rests in the One we call Savior and Friend. In such an unpredictable world, why would any sane chicken safely cross the road? Because she waddles beneath the shadow of much bigger wings.

He will cover you with his feathers, and under his wings you will find refuge; his faithfulness will be your shield and rampart. You will not fear the terror of night, nor the arrow that flies by day, nor the pestilence that stalks in the darkness.
Psalm 91:4-6

Safety Tips for Chicks on the Go

Chicken Nugget

1. Buy or borrow a cell phone.

2. Make sure the battery is fully charged.

3. Stock your glove compartment with a first aid kit, flashlight and batteries, and maps.

4. Keep your car manual in the car.

5. Know where to find the locking lug nut. You will need this to remove a flat tire.

6. Have a spare key and the locksmith code in your wallet or purse. (There is a number on a little silver tag that tells the locksmith how to make a new key to fit your car.)

7. In cold weather carry a candle and matches inside a coffee can in the trunk. This can serve as a tiny stove to keep you from freezing if you end up in a snowdrift.

8. Carry a sleeping bag or blanket in the trunk.

9. If you run into a wall or if your accelerator gets stuck, turn off the key.

10. Keep a screwdriver in the front part of the car. To break a window, place the point against the glass and hit the other end with the heel of your hand.

11. If you decide to drive through water, *go slowly.*

CHAPTER 14

Patchwork Perches

by Susan Duke

At 9:30 A.M. twenty ladies from a local church filed through my back door. Each brought a covered dish for lunch, and their eyes danced with anticipation as they made their way to the coffee pot and muffins. I encouraged them to tour the house (like women love to do) and then find a comfortable place in the living room before our day retreat began.

I noticed one of the ladies, Joan, seemed quite intrigued with all the quilts hanging across the log railing in the loft. "Did you make all of these?" she asked.

"Oh no," I laughed, "these are antique quilts—from the eighteen hundreds or early nineteen hundreds."

"Do you have any you've made yourself?" she continued.

"No, I don't sew."

"You don't? I'm really surprised," Joan remarked.

"I just admire them . . . and the people who made them." I explained. "I gave up on sewing after I had a horrible experience in a junior high homemaking class." The curious look on her face let me know I was going to have to explain:

I hated everything about sewing, from cutting out the pattern to threading the machine. I had no patience or concept of how all the pieces fit together. While I was enchanted with the possibility of actually making a garment I could wear, I was terrified at how it might turn out—and with good reason!

I'll never forget the day the teacher instructed us to sew up the seams to our dresses and then go to the cloakroom, one by one, try on our finished dress, and model it for the rest of the class. When I got to the cloakroom and started to slip my dress over my head, I was horrified to find I had sewn up the entire neck. My hands were barely sticking out the sleeve openings and my beautiful blue dress fit like a puckered paper sack pulled over my head! As pitifully as you can imagine, I whined, "Miss Belew, I can't come out." But she insisted. As I slowly opened the door and groped my way out the door, hysterical laughter filled the room.

"I don't think that will work, Miss Tussey," quipped my stoic homemaking teacher, also regarded as "a master seamstress." (She made three-piece gabardine suits in one night and wore them proudly to class the next day.) "I can't even guess what you've done to that dress!"

There was no way to explain that sewing was as foreign to me as car repair. I was almost in tears, knowing an entire semester grade was literally resting on my head. I turned to go and get dressed while the laughter continued. When the bell rang and class was dismissed, I felt I'd been let out of prison. I never wanted to see the inside of that classroom again!

As I was walking out of the room, my teacher caught me and said, "I just want you to know, I'm going to pass you in spite of your failure on this project. You've tried hard in my class, and I think perhaps you're not cut out (pardon the pun) for sewing. So, I'm giving you a D— instead of an F . . . go, enjoy life, you're free."

I was relieved and grateful. And I have never tried my hand at sewing again. I can design curtains, and even tell my husband (whose Granny taught him to sew) how to make them, but I can't make them myself. Choir members in my church were shocked one Easter to find out that Harvey had made the majestic purple costume I wore in the Easter cantata. Perhaps it's because of my struggle and inadequacies with sewing that I so admire people who have mastered it.

When I look at a homemade quilt the first thing I think of is the effort and long hours spent to create a lovely heirloom. And I especially love old quilts— really old quilts—quilts that have survived the ravages of time. It's not just the colors, design, and unique feel of these masterpieces that capture my heart, but rather, the stories, the lives that the quilt represents. I can't help but wonder about the person who created each one, sitting for hours piecing together scraps from outgrown clothing, perhaps an old apron or a work shirt or dress—one block at a time. Who were these women who stitched together such works of art, using fragments from the fabric of their lives?

When Joan continued to ask about my quilt collection, she wanted to know the names of all the patterns and where they originated. I was happy to share some of what I'd learned while researching antique quilts in preparation for a business speech I had to give.

I learned that names and quilt pattern ideas were most often birthed from images women observed in their surroundings. Isolated during the long winter months, they found their inspiration in things as simple as a flock of geese, flying in a V formation overhead, or the flames leaping in the fireplace. Such is the case in the popular log cabin design, with its bright red, orange, or yellow center square representing the fire; long strips of fabric sewn in rows on both sides of the center depicting the logs; and variations of light colors on one side of the square and dark colors on the other representing the shadows that the fire casts upon cabin walls.

In simpler times, beautiful craftsmanship was highly regarded—especially in quilting circles. The most uniform and tiniest of stitches were the marks of a fine quilt maker. Special recognition was often bestowed upon the best or perfect quilter. Christian women who guarded their hearts from pride deliberately left one plain, colorless block in their quilts that stood out from the rest. This one block portrayed a humble message—that nothing is perfect except God.

For most women today, isolation is a thing of the past. Instead our lives are filled with great waves of going and doing. There are jobs, carpools, luncheons, shopping, decorating, and so forth. Nevertheless, it is interesting to think about what kind of quilts would best represent the days of our lives. What patterns would we choose to illustrate our turning points and our memories? Would we have the courage to celebrate the pain along with the joy?

I've often wondered what type of quilt I would design to celebrate the friendships in my life. It certainly would be unique in color and design. First, I'd cut little patchwork perches—branches with heart shaped leaves. Then I'd design colorfully feathered hens of various sizes, colors, personalities, and expressions. I might embroider their names and a descriptive word above each perch.

When I looked at my quilt, I'd see Brenda, Joanna, LeAnn, Bettie, Charlet, Susie, Janice, Mary, Marla, Cathy, Jackie, Judy, Sue, Sandy, Juanelle, Cheryl, Berta, Sonja, Nell, Joy, Rosie, and so many others who have given my life so much gladness, hospitality, humor, concern, truthfulness, support, and acceptance.

And there is one more thing I would do with my friendship quilt. Within its borders, I'd create a unique portrayal of huddled hens sitting in a circle, lovingly scratching out words like courage, grace, love, perseverance, loyalty, and mercy. Above their perches I'd embroider the names of four nurturing hens named Becky, Fran, Rebecca, and Gracie.

During our hen gatherings as we've sat around a table, patching together pieces of our lives into story blocks, creating a greater message than any one of us might have done alone, I'm mindful of the beautiful patchwork quilt that covers my life. A collection of colorful, slightly irregular, and brightly colored blocks, intricately woven together, display a precious coverlet of nurturing friends . . . friends who don't care if you sew up all the wrong seams. Friends who cover my heart with a blanket of love.

And I can't help but think back to junior high and how even though I should have failed, one teacher's grace allowed me to pass anyway. I like to think of that block in my life's quilt as the one that reminds me that nothing is perfect except God. And that it's the Master Quilter, with golden threads of mercy, Who pardons me from my failures, as He takes the tattered scraps of my life and turns them into works of art.

And then, just because He loves me, He gives me a passing grade.

Two are better than one,
because they have a good return for their work:
If one falls down,
his friend can help him up. . . .
Also, if two lie down together, they will keep warm.
But how can one keep warm alone?
Ecclesiastes 4:9-11

Chicken Nugget

"How many, many friendships life's path has let me see;
I've kept a scrap of each of them to make the whole
of me."

June Masters Bacher

CHAPTER 15

The Henhouse Hospital for Wounded Chicks

by Fran Caffey Sandin

"What do you mean by that?" Carrie retorted.

"We've never done it that way and we are not going to start now," Lisa countered.

A troubling problem emerged in a women's church group I attended years ago. During a planning meeting, two ladies battled with words. Perhaps they had forgotten to take their hormone pills, their panty hose were too tight, or they needed a strong dose of chocolate. Whatever the cause, the issue certainly did not merit the Sherman tank approach that ensued.

As we women will sometimes do, the remaining group members quickly jumped into the fray and began snipping at each other. The results? After a few rounds of angry ammunition and a big explosion, we left the meeting looking like cartoon characters with all our feathers blown completely off. Only a few wisps of down remained.

My usual response to disagreements was to duck into a corner and pout, or cry a little, then get back to work. With my "peace at any price" disposition, I usually steered clear of arguments. But as

I continued to reflect upon the unfortunate incident involving cherished friends, I felt a strong nudge to step in and help. Me? Handle conflicts? No way. I wanted to hide.

The next morning when the phone rang, our leader, Carrie, tearfully said, "I don't know what to do, Fran. It might be best if I resign."

"No," I declared with an air of authority that surprised me. "You're doing a great job. I think you and Lisa need to work things out."

"I just feel terrible about the whole thing," Carrie explained. "Maybe if I step aside, everyone will be happier."

"No, Carrie," I admonished. "If you leave, hurt feelings will remain. We need a resolution to all this." I just couldn't let the friction continue to divide our group. So I organized a face-to-face meeting in my home the following day, realizing that I had no choice but to open my own ICC Unit (Intensive Coop Care).

When I phoned Willene, she questioned, "Are you sure it's a good idea to meet so soon? Maybe we need more time."

Paula and Lisa also hedged, and I had to convince them, too.

By the time I got to Dottie, I was short on patience. "Dottie," I said sternly, "if you don't come, I'm calling 911 and sending the ambulance out to bring you here." Finally everyone agreed to attend.

The following day, I arose early, added the finishing touches on my preparations, and paused to ask God for a LOT of help.

As the gals arrived, the tense atmosphere felt like a thousand fingernails scratching down a blackboard—nothing like the fun gatherings we'd enjoyed in the past. As we sat around my kitchen table, we all looked like wounded chicks—singed feathers drooping, beaks curled down at the corners.

After I'd read a few selected verses from the Bible, the atmosphere seemed to soften. Then—one by one—we began to open up.

Carrie spoke first, "Lisa, I know that part of the problem has been my attitude toward you. I'm so sorry. Will you please forgive me?"

A misty-eyed Lisa responded with a nod. Then the walls came crumbling down. We exchanged our chicken hearts for new and deeper dimensions of friendship as we talked for the next hour, giving and receiving apologies and forgiveness. Through bold but loving confrontation, healing had begun.

"I'll be right back," I said as I dashed off to the bedroom to stage my grand finale. While the others enjoyed coffee and brownies, I donned a nurse's uniform. A white nurse's cap, huge gold disk earrings that dangled almost to my shoulders, a long shirt with a stethoscope printed on the front, white shorts, thick socks pulled up to my knees, and tennis shoes completed the ensemble. I carried an antique black doctor's bag filled with chocolate candy and Nurse Franny Bananny's Remedies.

Before entering the kitchen, I paused and struck a dramatic pose in the doorway—a grand entrance that shocked my friends. None of them suspected this serious-minded hen had a playful bone in her body. Then everyone began laughing—sidesplitting, knee-slapping guffaws—especially when I read the correctives for our ailments.

GRAND OPENING!
THE HYSTERICAL HENHOUSE HOSPITAL
FOR WOUNDED CHICKS
Specializing in:
Cackle-rite for Mad Hen Disease

Crutches for Walking on Eggs

Roller Brushes for Cocked Combs

Cornatrol for Aching Gizzards

Liposuction for Prickly Quills

Feather Lifts for Downy Droop

Mega TLC for Hug-starved Chicks

Bleach-out for Blue Birds

Corn-Start for Mental Pause

Washumout Cluck for Fowl Language

Bandages for Smashed Egos

Sweet Pellets for Sour Gullets

Regularly Scheduled Chocolate Feedings
for Chick PMS and Other Related Disorders

When the hoopla settled, we ate our chocolates and ended the day with freedom. We had established stepping stones to healing, restored fellowship, and renewed trust. By forgiving one another, we loved our friends even more. All in all, we had a great time and, as a bonus, I gained confidence in handling conflicts.

But, let me make one thing perfectly clear—we still need regular doses of chocolate.

A cheerful heart does good like medicine,
but a broken spirit makes one sick.
Proverbs 17:22 TLB

Chicken Nugget

The Medical Profession Acknowledges the Following Benefits of Humor:

Summarized from "Therapeutic Use of Humor"
by Linda Schickedanz, BSN, RN
DFW NURSING, August, 1992, pp. 14,15

1. Boosts immune system
2. Stimulates circulation
3. Releases endorphines (to reduce pain and cause a sense of well-being)
4. Decreases pulse and blood pressure
5. Stimulates respiration
6. Relieves tension
7. Decreases anxiety and stress
8. Relieves embarrassment
9. Enhances memory, learning, creativity
10. Creates feelings of acceptance and teamwork
11. Serves as an outlet for hostility and anger
12. Facilitates interaction and decreases social distance
13. Releases tension from social conflicts
14. Relieves the burden of reality

CHAPTER 16

Teatime Hens

by Susan Duke

We met over a bouquet of flowers.

When Cathy, a charming pastor's wife, saw some floral arrangements I'd made for a local shop, she asked the shop owner for my name and number. A few days later, Cathy called to see if I would create an arrangement for her church. She seemed concerned about the details; but I assured her if she could tell me the size, colors, and type of container she wanted, I would design something she'd be pleased with.

When the arrangement was finished, I called to ask if she could meet me at the church. I arrived just as Cathy was unlocking the glass door. Her eyes danced with anticipation as she invited me in. When I placed the arrangement on the foyer table, she clapped her hands like a happy little girl. She loved the wedgewood blue, deep rose, burgundy, and parchment colors of the silk and dried flowers that graced the brass urn.

"It's just perfect!" she said excitedly. "I can't believe it's just the way I had it pictured in my mind. I may have you make several more—one for each season."

We said our good-byes and I left, not knowing if I would hear from Cathy again. But about a month later, she called to order a large burgundy Christmas arrangement in a basket, careful to allow plenty of time before the holiday season arrived. This time, when I'd finished the arrangement, she asked if she and her husband, Bobby, could come and pick it up. Once again, she was delighted with the finished product.

Several days later, Cathy phoned again. "The reason I'm calling," she said, "is to see if you might be free for lunch." We agreed on a time for the next day.

At the restaurant, we exchanged small talk while we waited for our orders. Then Cathy paused and softly, yet emphatically, said, "You may think this is strange, but I've felt comfortable with you from the first time I met you, and I've decided you're going to be my friend whether you want to be or not!" We chuckled warmly, but her expression stilled as she continued. "I need a friend," she confided. "And you seem so upbeat and happy, like someone I'd like to get to know."

A friendship was born that day and as time went on, we began meeting once a month for lunch at a tearoom. We challenged ourselves to find a new tearoom each time we had our "girl's day out." Once we were on the way to our destination, we giggled like two little girls determined to have fun and play as long as time would allow.

We soon dubbed ourselves the "tearoom critics." And I must say, we've had some pretty hilarious adventures, most within a sixty-mile radius of our hometown. We discovered early on that some tearooms are tearooms in name only. Like the one in a small neighboring town, where several old men in overalls were sitting around playing dominoes, chewing tobacco, and using language that would never be tolerated in proper company. Still, we decided we were hungry, so we stayed. When we ordered chicken salad from the menu, we were told they were already sold out, even though it was barely noon.

The waitress quipped, "How 'bout tuna? We always got plenty of that."

"Well, okay," we replied reluctantly.

Soon our perky waitress came whistling her way back to our table, tuna plates in hand. I looked at Cathy and she looked at me as our lunch was set before us. Our tuna special was served on dry scorched toast, spread with mustard and a side order of broken potato chips.

We were instructed to get our own tea from the jar on a wobbly half-painted white table. The huge mugs we picked up were thick with dust, and it was evident the tea had been "steeping" for more than awhile. When we asked for a cup of hot tea, the waitress quickly pointed out that "hot" tea was not on the brown-stained handwritten menu.

Despite our less than delightful luncheon, we were excited about browsing through the twelve quaint little shops we had been told we could find nearby. But once again, we were disappointed when our vision of shops bordering the town square turned out to be three rows of long shelves—each filled with flea market items.

Stunned with disappointment and dazed with hunger, we barely made it to the car before we broke out into one of those take-your-breath-away, deep belly laughs—the kind that leaves you begging for mercy and loving every moment of it.

We drove another twenty miles to a nearby town (where we probably should have gone in the first place), and found a bonafide tearoom where we treated ourselves to coffee latté and a chocolate gourmet dessert.

The day's adventure inspired us to keep individual "tearoom" journals, where we would record our tearoom get-togethers, critique the places we visited, and then read what we'd written over lunch the following month. As Cathy read her evaluation of our last lunch meeting and then I read mine, we were amazed to hear how they coincided.

About a year later, I called Cathy one day to see how she'd been. We were both extremely busy and hadn't touched base in awhile. She was overloaded with church projects and her job, and I was on a writing deadline, along with a full load of speaking dates. She sounded stressed and said she was taking the day off. I detected a bit of melancholy in her voice and wondered if she could use some cheering up.

"If you're going to be home, I may just pop in later and say hello," I said before hanging up the phone. Then, I heated some water in my teakettle, got two dainty teacups from my antique cupboard, and packed them in a picnic basket. When the teakettle whistled, I found some loose herbal tea in my pantry called "Hops." I hadn't yet tried this particular blend, but the label lauded its wonderful "calming" properties. *Just what Cathy needs,* I thought, putting several scoops in a pan and pouring hot water over them. After steeping and straining, I poured the bubbly liquid into a blue thermos carafe and hurried off with the perfect prescription to brighten a sister hen's day.

When Cathy answered the door, she seemed reserved and quiet, yet pleasantly surprised to see me carrying a picnic basket. "You don't have to do anything," I assured her. "Let's just go to your garden room table and have a tea party—just like old times." Her winsome smile told me she was grateful and touched by my concern.

After I poured the steaming tea, we sat with both hands folded around our teacups, waiting for the aroma to find our noses. We weren't giggly or giddy, and we didn't even need to talk—all we needed was a friendship break.

We waited anxiously for the tea to cool slightly, and then, picked up our cups and took long sips. As I struggled to swallow the green liquid swimming in my mouth, I glanced across the table at Cathy's grimaced face. Something was dreadfully wrong! We gulped and coughed in unison.

"What is this stuff?" Cathy blurted.

"Well, well . . . I don't know exactly! I thought it was a great, relaxing gourmet tea called 'Hops,'" I stammered. "I hoped it would de-stress you!"

"More sugar?" Kathy pleaded looking my way. We were determined to have our tea. But once again, we nearly gagged. There was absolutely nothing we could do to make this horribly bitter tea drinkable.

Suddenly, Cathy began to giggle and soon her giggles gave way to uproarious laughter.

We didn't even notice when Cathy's husband, Bobby, came home. When we spotted him standing there watching us "whoop it up," we tried to regain control. But it was too late.

"What in the world are you two drinking?" he asked.

"We think it's tea—a special calming tea," we explained gasping for air.

"It doesn't seem to be calming anyone down," he responded, "but it's awfully good to see Cathy laughing."

We poured the last drops of tea down the sink. We hugged, and then I went on my way thinking about how a blessing had turned into a disaster, but the disaster had made the day a blessing.

Of all the teatimes we've spent and will spend in the future, we'll always remember how our friendship was nurtured by a "tearoom blue plate special," and how bitter tea brought sweet laughter to our souls.

I have great boldness and free and fearless confidence and
cheerful courage toward you; my pride in you is great.
I am filled [brimful] with the comfort [of it]; with all
our tribulation and in spite of it, [I am filled with
comfort] I am overflowing with joy.
2 Corinthians 7:4 AMP

Chicken Nugget

Friendship is like a cup of tea.
Steeped in the warmth of sharing,
its potion fills us up,
soothes our spirits, and sweetens our lives with joy.

CHAPTER 17

Chicks in Dixie

by Becky Freeman

In my travels through states like Alabama, Georgia, Mississippi, Kentucky, and Tennessee, I had a revelation of sorts. Though I'd always considered myself a true GRITS (Girl Raised in the South), I came to see there are several small differences between Texas "South," and Deep South "South."

First, there's the Southern drawl. Like our Southern sisters, we also pronounce three-letter words using four distinct syllables, but we Texas gals tend to lean on our "Rs" rather than ignore their existence. We "linger" a hair longer at the end of a word, rather than "linguh" on the first syllable the way they do in Dixie. (As an aside: Ann Barrett Batson says Southerners don't drawl because they're lazy. It's because the words taste good.)

Then, there is the issue of speed. Though folks from Dallas and Houston and San Antonio certainly mosey through life at a much slower pace than New Yorkers, we haven't yet mastered the Southern art of loungin' and lollin' around, to relax in near-liquid form in a porch swing or hammock. I have to admit, my friends from the Deep South are gourmet relaxers. They know how to meander, recline—even rest in sweet repose. So when I need to press the pause button on my fast-forward life, I head to antebellum territory, gratefully humming, "I've got friends in slow places."

Such was the case when I flew to Tennessee recently. I was scheduled to speak at a women's conference along with fellow author and friend, Lindsey O'Conner (who flew into Nashville from her home in Colorado). Both of us are busy wives and moms with four children apiece; and we were both facing tough writing deadlines. To make matters worse, we were also more than a little nervous about finding the conference center, two hours away, on this dark Friday night. By the time we hugged each other at the airport, our stress was approaching near panic level. It didn't take long for us to realize, however, that nobody in Nashville seemed harried. In fact, quite the opposite.

After gathering our luggage, we climbed aboard a Hertz™ van that would take us to our rental car. The driver, a friendly fellow named Buck, insisted on loading every piece of our luggage (much of it packed to a back-breaking brim with our books). As soon as we, along with our fellow passengers, settled in our places, Buck made the rounds, shaking hands with every person in his charge.

"Glad to meet you; nice to have you aboard," Buck said with a smile. Then just before taking the driver's seat, he cheerfully declared, "I never ride with strangers." I half expected him to don a cardigan and sing, "It's a Beautiful Day in the Neighborhood."

"I love the South," I replied, relaxing into a deep Southern twang. Here in the lap of Dixie, surrounded by Tennessee strangers, who acted more like aunts and uncles, my neck muscles were already beginning to loosen up.

We arrived at the women's conference just in time. The weekend progressed beautifully, the attendees welcomed us warmly, and God's presence was sweet and near. The leaves, at the height of their autumn color, gave our surroundings a golden-red glow. By late Saturday afternoon, the conference was over, and I drove through quaint towns and farms as Lindsey relaxed in the passenger seat.

We'd each spoken three times in the last twenty-four hours, plus nonstop visiting with women who'd been energized by two days away from husbands, kids, dishes, and laundry. The only thing Lindsey and I now had the energy to verbalize was an occasional, "Oh, there's a pretty tree." We actually passed the first few hours by practicing synchronized yawning in a silent ballet of mutual exhaustion.

After a few miles, Lindsey found the strength to form a complete sentence. "I know we were thinking about heading to a hotel, Becky, but what we really need is a Southern mother, a home-cooked meal, and a good night's sleep."

"Ye-up," I answered, not yet up to full talkin' speed. I surmised that not only sleepiness, but the South itself had now taken hold of my tongue and slowed it to well below the national speed limit.

"What we need is a Posy," Lindsey continued with rising energy.

"A what?" I asked, now curious.

"How far are we from Murray, Kentucky?" Lindsey asked. We checked a map and discovered we were only a few miles from Murray, where Lindsey's old friend Posy lived. They had met years back while doing a radio show about home-based businesses.

"I think I'll give her a call," Lindsey said, speaking like a woman on a mission to find a refuge of homemade hospitality.

"Posy?" she said into the cellular phone. "My friend Becky and I are in your neck of the woods, and we are badly in need of some pampering."

I grinned as Lindsey finished the conversation and hung up the phone. "Get ready, girl. We're headin' to a real Southern kitchen for some good old-fashioned stress relief."

My stomach growled at the thought of home-cooked food.

We pulled up to a sprawling ranch-style home, and Posy, the picture of a gracious Southern mother (apron firmly attached), opened the front door and greeted us. "Hello, theuh, gals! Y'all come in out of that weathuh and get warm now."

Luscious smells poured from the kitchen all the way down the hallway. We dined that evening on parmesan chicken, green bean salad, pineapple sweet potato casserole, and flaky heart-shaped biscuits. After friendly conversation and a tour of Posy's cross-stitching business, our hostess appeared with a fresh coconut cake and hot coffee. We'd landed in Kentucky "slowdown" heaven, and I wondered how I'd find the will to venture out onto life's fast forward highway again.

The next morning I woke refreshed, feeling like the Queen of the Great South as I stretched lazily in a quilt-covered poster bed. After slipping on a soft, comfy robe, I passed Lindsey in the hall on the way to the restroom. Adopting my best Georgia drawl, I leaned against the wall with a sigh. "Can we go out on the verandah, sip our mint tea, and watch the grass grow now?" I asked wistfully. Lindsey nodded, a relaxed smile lighting up her pretty, well-rested face.

Oh, how we women need to take time out to renew our batteries and fill our emotional and spiritual tanks, I thought as I meandered back toward the guest room a few minutes later. How often had I turned down precious opportunities to get away and relax in the past? Why had I not taken advantage of more moments like this? In part, I think it was because I thought that taking a break was shirking my responsibilities.

But the older I get, the more I realize that my children would rather have a rested, happy momma who takes some time for replenishment, than a nonstop supermom who eventually grows to be as cranky as an old wet hen. I also discovered, to my great surprise, that Scott and the kids coped amazingly well with my occasional absence to enjoy a "mental health" day.

I fluffed up the pillows, reached for a good book, and sank back onto the quilt coverlet, willing all thoughts of projects and pressures to be gone with the wind. In the spirit of the silver screen's most famous Southern belle, I decided to simply think about those things tomorrow. After all, if I was going to "linguh" here in the deep South, I wanted to unwind like a native: slo-o-o-o-wly and gracefully, savoring each moment.

Come to me, all you who are weary and
burdened, and I will give you rest.
Matthew 11:28

Chicken Nugget

From
Everyday Sacred
by Susan Bender

Mine is a racehorse rhythm,
and once I get started . . .
it's difficult for me to stop.
Now I can see that a pause—even a very
small pause—is extremely useful.
These "little Sabbaths" replenish
my body—and spirit.

SECTION III

Chickens on Parade

Courage When Celebrating Life's Special Moments

CHAPTER 18

Blue Hen Party

by Becky Freeman

It was near Thanksgiving, but I was feeling far from thankful. We'd just had our second baby in two years, and Scott had started a new construction business. The bad thing about the construction business is that it's so dependent on the weather, and the bad thing about the weather is that it is so undependable. Weeks of rain had taken its toll on our family mood and budget.

One afternoon I put the boys down for a nap, never an easy trick for me. Catching two wide-awake little boys felt a lot like trying to herd baby chicks. After changing their diapers, nursing Zeke, and reading *Pat the Bunny* six times, I was often so exhausted I'd collapse on the bed just to recover from the ordeal of their nap time.

But this afternoon I'd managed to stay awake—and aware. Aware that we had no money. Our checking account was dwindling fast and every dollar had to be counted and stretched. No matter what anyone says about the dignity and challenges of being poor, believe me, it's no fun. Worrisome thoughts tumbled through my mind, one on top of the other. *How will we buy groceries? What about Christmas presents? Will we be able to pay our bills? Will we ever be able to afford a night out again?*

I was in the middle of a full-blown pity party. And then, I hatched a novel idea. Surely I wasn't the only person feeling like a boneless chicken in this season of plump, festive turkey dinners. I could expand this bleak experience of mine to include other out-of-work friends. I could invite people to come to my pity party!

Parties always got my motor going. I went to the kitchen and took out a big brown grocery sack, sat down at the dining room table, then tore it into 5 x 5 inch squares. On each square I wrote:

"You are invited to a Hard Luck Party. Come as you are. Nothing is too ragged for this social event. Bring a package of whatever cheap luncheon meat you can afford, and we'll make a five-foot-long poor-boy sandwich. Be prepared to share a hard luck story with the rest of us, and do your best to make it as pitiful sounding as possible; we all need cheering up."

Then I wrote the time, date, and location, and put a stamp on the back of each homemade "brown sack" invitation.

It's been twenty years since that party, and to this day my friends still talk about how much fun it was. Instead of cleaning up for the occasion, I actually stirred up the disorder in my already cluttered house. The pictures hung askew on the walls, kids' toys lay scattered everywhere, the curtains were draped and looped in mass disarray. The men arrived dressed in ragged T-shirts or overalls, the women in old, faded cotton dresses that hung loose and limp. The children were adorned in pillowcases and paper bags—whatever old thing their parents found laying around.

When it came time to share our "hard luck" stories, the room exploded in laughter. Each couple exaggerated the dire urgency of their circumstance to ridiculous, pitiful proportions. At one point, one of the men reached for an old guitar and with a sad Southern accent, began to sing an impromptu ballad of despondency. "Poor and tired and pitiful ol' me, I'm drowning in a sea of misery. . . ."

We carried on like a bunch of whinin' hound dogs, singing one sad song after another until we felt great. Of all the parties I've ever given, this one beats them all—not because it was creative or well-planned or special, but because we so desperately needed to laugh, to empathize, to not feel alone in our situation. The comfort of a common bond is one of God's greatest ways to strengthen discouraged hearts.

I have a friend and neighbor, Ethel Sexton, who is what we country folk call "an absolute hoot." One day I heard what sounded like a bunch of chickens squawking and carrying on outside my front door. I looked at my daughter and said, "What's that?"

She peeked out the window and said, "Mom, it's Ethel. She's talking to Daddy in the driveway.

Ethel doesn't just talk, she *enthusiates.* Though Ethel came from a childhood where money was scarce as hen's teeth, she will tell you in a heartbeat that her childhood was rich. Ethel takes her message of joy all over the country, and every day she delivers a two-minute radio spot for KCBI here in the Dallas-Fort Worth area. She ends every show with a classic sign-off: "This is Ethel Sexton, reminding you to make your O-O-O-OWN SUNSHINE!"

In other words, when life gives you a bad turn, turn it into a party. When it rains, make your own "indoor sunshine." Not long ago I had a chance to put Ethel's motto to the test.

It was the first year I'd actually made a profit from my writing. So I splurged, reserving a beach house for a sun-splashed week in Gulf Shores, Alabama. How our family anticipated those long, lazy days of nothing but sunshine. None of us were emotionally prepared for seven long, lazy days of nonstop rain.

In my whole life, I do not remember it raining for seven days straight—not anywhere, anytime, or for any reason. Why did this have to happen during our one precious week of vacation? Each day I would walk out on the "sun deck" to watch a new storm gathering. *"Oh, Lord,"* I'd whine with the fervency of a child begging for candy, *"please, just a bit of blue. Just a shimmer of sun. Please, God, please."* Then with a clap of thunder, I'd get my unwanted answer. "Not today, child, not today."

When it finally occurred to me that the rain might never stop, that we might actually have to go home in an ark, I began to look in other directions for sunshine. One afternoon, I headed to the grocery store, purchasing party supplies, a big fluffy cake sprinkled with confetti-like candy, candles, some cheap toy favors, and the best part of all—a bouquet of sunny yellow balloons.

When I drove up the driveway to the beach house, Scott met me coming down the stairs.

"What have you done?" he asked, eyeing the bobbing balloons.

"We're going to have a party. I'm making my O-O-O-OWN SUNSHINE!"

Scott laughed and said, "I was just coming to tell you, I ran down the beach a little while ago and brought you the sun."

"See!" he said, pointing skyward like a boy showing off the puppy that followed him home.

Sure enough, between two clouds, a sliver of sunshine peeked through, pouring out light that shimmered like liquid diamond dust. Then Scott gestured toward the sky above the ocean, and the sight was so magnificent I felt tears sting my eyes. Using the mist of the rain, and that bit of sun, God had created a full rainbow for our viewing pleasure.

And it dawned on me then that God does not waste the rain in our lives. For without the rain, ultimately, our lives would be colorless. We'd be less appreciative, less compassionate people. We survive the rainy days by trusting the Son to shine from the inside out—by making our own sunshine in life's darkest corners. And finally, because there has been rain, the sun can paint a glorious rainbow.

And so, the same is true in our hearts.

> *Whenever the rainbow appears in the clouds, I will*
> *see it and remember the everlasting covenant.*
> Genesis 9:16

Chicken Nugget

From
O Love That Wilt Not Let Me Go
Words, George Matheson, 1882
Tune St. Margaret, Albert L. Peace, 1884
(Information from *Baptist Hymnal*,
Convention Press, Nashville, TN, 1975)

O Joy that seekest me through pain,

I cannot close my heart to thee;

I trace the rainbow through the rain,

And see the promise is not vain

That morn shall tearless be.

CHAPTER 19

Peck the Halls

by Gracie Malone

For weeks I'd looked like a brown-haired version of Martha Stewart as I planned and organized "the perfect family holiday." On Christmas Eve, the tree glistened with new lights and ornaments fastened to the tip of each branch. Dozens of carefully selected gifts wrapped in color-coordinated paper nestled in the folds of the handmade quilted skirt. The dining table was laden with goodies and adorned with silk poinsettias and gold ribbon. My preparations complete, I wiped my hands on my apron, poured myself a cup of coffee, and waited for the kids to arrive. As I sipped the warm flavorful brew, I thought, *This will be the most perfect Christmas ever.*

Before long, our son, Matt, and the first brood of grandchicks bolted through the back door. Then Mike and his family parked at the curb out front, and Jason, our youngest, roared up in his Z-28. After a round of boisterous hugs, Joe and I helped them unload their cars and moved the celebration indoors.

Soon our three-bedroom house was stuffed like a Christmas turkey. Nobody seemed to notice the decorations, as thirteen people, including six kids from two months to nine years old, pushed into the space usually occupied by two semi-retired adults and one lazy dachshund. They had come from afar, bearing gifts—and packing two duffel bags, four kid-sized sleeping bags, four backpacks, two diaper bags, four cots, two porta-cribs, one high chair, one bouncer chair, a stack of blankets, two mega-packs of diapers, and one hamper full of dirty laundry.

Mike removed the cinnamon-flavored candle and evergreen ring from the center of the coffee table, plopped the infant seat down, and placed baby Myles in his rightful place as center of attention. Montana, an active three-year-old, jumped in our rocking recliner and rode it like a bucking bronco. Luke, Connor, and Mary Catherine zipped around the Christmas tree heading toward the garden room where they plowed through a basket of old toys, while twenty-one-month-old Abby ate candy from the dish on the end table. "She'll ruin her supper!" I shouted as I scooped her into my arms and headed for the dining room.

Abby wasn't the only one thinking about food. We gathered at the table and gobbled up so much smoked turkey and trimmings I thought we'd never be hungry again. But I no sooner got the kitchen cleaned up, closed down, and declared off limits, than I heard Matt rummaging through the refrigerator. "Mom, got any cheese and Ro-tel™ tomatoes?" As I searched through the pantry, I thought about the cheese ball and dainty crackers I'd planned to serve after the kids went to bed. Then I rolled up my sleeves, and started cooking. For the next half hour, we stood around the stove dipping tortilla chips into melted cheese while the kids watched a Christmas video.

When we joined them in the living room, Montana jumped out of the chair and, in a voice that commanded everybody's attention, yelled, "Wait! I've gotta go." When all eyes turned his direction, he shrugged his shoulders, turned his palms up, and said, "I've got to have some milk, that's all." As he trudged toward the kitchen, I shook my head and prayed that my old refrigerator would keep humming through the holidays.

A few hours later, we bathed the kids, dressed them in warm footed pajamas, and gathered in the living room for our traditional story time. While the other kids scrambled for a place to sit, Montana climbed in my lap and examined the brass pendant hanging on a chain around my neck. It depicted the nativity scene, complete with the Holy Family and two members of the heavenly host.

In typical preschool fashion, he started asking questions. "Grandma Gracie, who is that man?"

"Why, that's Joseph," I answered.

"Well, who is that girl?" he asked pointing to the tiny woman seated in the straw.

"Her name is Mary. She's the mother. . . ."

"And who is that tiny little baby?"

"That, my precious grandchild, is Baby Jesus, God's own Son. He came from Heaven and was born in a manger."

"What's a manger? And, why is the star sooooo big? And. . . ." He took a huge gulp of air; then, with eyes wide in amazement and wonder, pointed to two angels hovering near the star, and asked, "Who are those guys?"

"Oh, Montana, those are angels. Two of the strongest dudes in God's army. They came to tell the shepherds about the Baby and to watch over Him while He was sleeping."

He responded with a simple, "Oh!" But, as I hugged him and helped him off my lap, I felt strangely warmed. It seemed as if the old, old story had taken on a new sort of freshness.

In that unplanned moment, Montana and I had redis-
covered the true meaning of the season. I shifted to the front
of my chair and reached for my mug of cider as our Papa Joe
began to read the Christmas story from the Bible, "I bring you
good news of great joy that will be for all the people. Today in
the town of David, a Savior has been born to you; He is Christ
the Lord." My heart filled with joy as I observed everyone
listening carefully. I remembered another occasion a few years
before when we'd gathered in the same room, told the same
story, and experienced the same unexpected joy.

After Joe read the Christmas story, Luke, four at the time,
decided to perform. He positioned himself smack in the middle
of the family circle and belted out the words of his favorite
song, "Rudolph the Red-Nosed Reindeer." Connor, our dimpled
toddler, sang along one syllable behind his older brother. It was
a stellar performance right down to the last phrase, "You'll go
down in hisss-stor-eeeeee." Doting family members responded
with an outburst of applause. Then, with a dramatic flair that
would have made Pavarotti proud, Luke placed one arm across
his waist in front and one behind, bowed gracefully and said,
"Thank you very much, thank you very much." Connor spread
his arms widely, and cheered, "Tah, dah, bra-bo, bra-bo."

Later, as I tucked my darling grandchildren into bed and
whispered good night, I couldn't help but believe they would,
along with Rudolph, go down in "hisss-stor-eeeee." And I, their
grateful grandmother, will always be cheering them on, "Bra-
bo, bra-bo."

The next morning, just as the sun peeped over the fence,
six kids popped out of bed and headed for the Christmas tree.
Sleepy-eyed adults joined them, and soon we were sitting in a
circle munching sausage balls and warming our hands with

mugs of hot coffee. The tree tottered and swayed as Luke and Connor retrieved and distributed gifts.

In no time, the floor was covered with crumpled paper, empty boxes, pieces of ribbon, and assorted toy parts, until finally there was only one present left under the tree. Luke read the card, "To Gracie from Joe," as he plopped the big box in front of me.

What in the world can it be, I wondered. I looked up in time to see the twinkle in Joe's eye. "I hope you like what I got you," he said. I quickly reassured him, "Of course I will, I always do!" Everybody was watching as I took a deep breath and ripped off the paper.

When I saw what was in the box, I couldn't believe my eyes. It was a paper shredder. To be honest, it was simply *too mulch!* I pasted on a smile that would have convinced Santa himself and said, "Something I've always wanted, yes sir, something I would have never bought for myself! Thank you."

Later that evening, after one last feeding frenzy in the kitchen, it was time for everybody to load up and go home. After a dozen trips to the assorted cars out front, Matt came back in and surveyed the living room to see if he'd forgotten anything. Suddenly we heard sounds of a struggle in the hallway. Glancing in that direction, we saw Abby toddling down the hall, pushing my cherrywood valet from the guest room. We stood with our mouths open as she headed for the front door. Matt didn't crack a grin as he said, "That's right, baby, just put it in the back seat on top of everything else."

Before dark, the house was quiet and empty again. I thought, *This really was the most perfect Christmas ever, but not because of my plans. God's blessings made it so.*

In his heart a man plans his course,
but the LORD determines his steps.
Proverbs 16:9

Gracie's Sausage Balls

Chicken Nugget

1 lb. bulk sausage
2 cups Bisquick™ baking mix
2 cups grated cheddar cheese

Mix with pastry blender or dough hook. Shape into balls. May be stored in freezer and cooked a few at a time. Bake in a 350 degree oven for 20 minutes or until golden brown.

CHAPTER 20

Preened to Perfection

by Rebecca Barlow Jordan

The organist cued the bride's entrance, but the visiting minister had not yet signaled us to rise.

"It's time, it's time!" I muttered under my breath. "Why doesn't he tell us to stand?" Finally, in exasperation, I exclaimed to my mother-in-law, "I'm going to stand!" I dried my clammy hands on my pink, silk mother-of-the-bride dress and smiled, but as I turned toward the back of the church, my heart froze with disappointment. *Too late,* I thought. *We're too late. She's already coming. We waited too long!*

There, already halfway down the aisle on the arm of her tall, handsome father, strolled my youngest daughter, Jennifer. As she passed, I glanced toward the front of the sanctuary and saw her beloved groom. His eyes shone like diamonds, his smile radiating like a thousand twinkling lights. At that moment, nothing else seemed to matter. The groom stood waiting to receive his bride.

Missing Jennifer's grand entrance was a small thing, but mentally, I checked it off as the last of "Oh, me's"—things gone wrong in our wedding preparations.

My first mistake was trying to coordinate all the wedding details myself. We scrutinized the price tag of every scrap of fabric, every button, every piece of jewelry, every bite of cake, and every ounce of liquid—to fit a wedding budget that barely filled a piggy bank.

Jennifer and I had started checking off our suggested "to do list"(103 items) months before the July wedding; yet I still felt unprepared and anything but confident. After all, this was our first daughter to fly the coop.

The Texas sun was so hot, we could have popped corn on the sidewalk. I ordered so much cake, we could have served the New Testament multitude of "five thousand" easily—with more than twelve basketfuls left over! A nagging thought surfaced repeatedly: *Why didn't we save more money for this occasion?* (We were paying off our share of the "national college debt," that's why!)

At the rehearsal dinner, somewhere between the parmesan chicken and the cherry cheesecake, I leaned over and whispered to my husband Larry, "I think I left the steamer on over at the other church." I could see tomorrow's headlines: *"Scatterbrained Mother of the Bride Burns Down Neighboring Church Fellowship Center."* Saved. One of the bridesmaid's husbands, a policeman, offered to check it out. False alarm!

Later that night, Jennifer bounded into our bedroom. "Mom! Two of the bridesmaids' dresses were sewn on the wrong side of the fabric!" she wailed.

I tried to reassure her. "No one will notice." Inside my confidence wavered. *Would we make it through this ordeal?*

About 1:30 A.M. the phone rang again. A wandering grooms-man pleaded, "Do you know where my hotel is?" Somewhere between two and three o'clock we drifted back to sleep. A few hours later, someone was pounding on our door. *Maybe I left the steamer on,* I thought. *Maybe our house is on fire.* We had overslept on the morning of the wedding! Ten garbage sacks full of fresh English ivy were "growing" in our bathtub, and my sister-in-law had come to collect them for decorations. We stumbled around, and finally Larry left to help transport the ivy to the church.

Thirty minutes later, Larry called back. Some of our specially ordered "fuschia" roses had wilted in the refrigerator. "The bridesmaid flowers look like leftovers from last week's church funeral," he said. "But Jen's bouquet is fine." While Larry and our oldest daughter, Valerie, hunted for some new flowers, I ran to meet my friend to finish decorating the reception site and meet the cake lady.

By noon, we were scrambling to finish before the 3:00 wedding hour. I was overwhelmed and almost in tears, my worst fears unfolding. Would I be late to my daughter's wedding? I saw myself standing before the church, weeping and unprepared like the five foolish virgins who had no oil in Matthew 25. Would I disappoint my daughter and shatter her expectations as well as my own?

The phone on the kitchen wall of the church jangled my already frayed nerves. "Mom!" barked Valerie. "I'm locked out of the house, and it's 100 degrees out here!"

We converged at home to find Valerie on the front porch, looking more like a wet hen than a cheery bridesmaid. But soon we were dressed and on our way to the church.

Miraculously, my sister-in-law arranged the new flowers in record time. When the music started, I stood paralyzed on the stairs, holding my daughter's train. Something inside of me temporarily refused to let go of precious past memories. Like a mother hen fussing over her baby chick, I preened a few of

Jen's feathery hair strands to perfection, hugged her, then flew down the stairs and walked to my seat in a daze.

She's beautiful. Everything is beautiful, I thought, as I heaved a sigh and looked around at the flowers, the tulle-draped pedestals, and the candles, all standing at attention. *Oh no! I forgot to take my hormones and I have no tissues!*

Finally my body relaxed, and I felt God's Spirit nudging my heart. *In my penchant for perfection and my determination to please, had I failed to see what really mattered today? Which was more important? My expectations? Or the celebration itself?* When I looked again at the groom standing there proudly to receive his new bride, and as I listened to them repeat their wedding vows, I bowed my head and whispered with renewed confidence, "God, You're in control." Then I uttered the following solemn promise of my own:

"Though the flowers wilt and the cake falls; though the groomsmen vanish and the air-conditioning fails; though the organ miscues and there's no room to seat the family; though the tape warps and the soloist sings off key; though the punch spills and my mother can't come; though the camera breaks and my stockings run, even then, I will rejoice in the Lord!"

It has been more than three years since Jennifer's wedding. Several months ago, Valerie called to announce, "Mom, Dad, I'm engaged!" My first thought was, *How about eloping?* Perhaps with this wedding, I will be wiser and more focused. This time I will worry less and trust more. This time I will remember to take my hormone medication!

Family weddings remind me of a future celebration in Heaven that awaits every believer in Christ. Our concern then will not be, "Do we have enough food? Are the flowers fresh? Will everyone stand on cue?" Only the solemn union will

matter, as we hasten into the arms of our adoring Groom—
Christ Jesus Himself.

What a perfect wedding day that will be, when our hearts
are lit like candles with anticipation! How our spirits will cry
out with joy when the King approaches with pomp and
ceremony. We'll see the face of Jesus—like the brilliance of a
thousand twinkling lights—and hear Heaven's trumpet
announce the words: "Behold, here comes the Groom!"

It's a moment worth waiting for.

And if I go and prepare a place for you,
I will come back and take you to be with me.
John 14:3

Preparing for Your Child's Wedding

1. P's and Q's are important (prayer and quiet time). You'll need ample doses.

2. Remember to keep an eternal perspective. Ask yourself continually, "What's really important here?"

3. Enlist a wedding coordinator, or at least willing friends, to help. It's worth the money.

4. Plan ahead, and include plenty of margin. Overtaxed bodies mean overstressed minds and emotions.

5. Attend every wedding you can, and talk to other mother hens who have "been there and done that" before—and after—planning your child's wedding.

6. Reassure your daughter (or son) that you are there for them. Your positive attitude will be contagious.

7. Enjoy the moments—especially the wedding day. My daughter commented later, "For so much work, it was over so quickly. I'd like to go through it again—and this time enjoy every moment more."

CHAPTER 21

When Gifts Have Wings

by Susan Duke

It's here! I shouted inwardly, as I pulled the loosely rolled package from my post office box. Since we live in the boonies, my husband usually retrieves the mail on his way home from work. But when I'm expecting something special, I make the five-mile drive into our small town myself.

And now at last, the package I was anticipating had finally arrived. My hands trembled as I carried it to my car and sat it on the seat beside me. I was tempted to rip it open and peek inside, but I didn't dare disturb the contents without proper respect for its unveiling. I had no choice but to take it home, where, in privacy, my unpredictable emotions could have free reign.

I'd never experienced a moment like this. It was a "first." It was a new dimension in my life, a new beginning. It was a rainbow-after-the-rain, happy-and-sad-at-the-same-time moment. And it would forever mark a page in the journal of my heart.

When I finally got back home, I felt like I was moving in slow motion as I found a comfortable chair to sit in and began to open the package. But I couldn't sit still. I had to stand. Carefully, I removed the tape that sealed the plastic covering and pulled out three complimentary copies of *Home Life* magazine. Inside was the first story I'd ever written, the first story I'd ever sent to a publisher, and the first time I would ever see that story and my name in print.

I thought with amazement of the thousands of people that would actually be reading something I had poured onto paper from my heart. I was holding a miracle in my hands.

I had good reason to feel especially sensitive about the copies of the December issue I received that cold, blustery, November day. The story was about an uncanny dream I had had about a star on the first Christmas after losing our eighteen-year-old son, Thomas. I had told this story on speaking occasions when I was specifically asked to give my testimony. I often referred to it as "my star story." Many times people asked if I had it written down and commented that they would like to share it with others. I always said, "No, but one day I will write it."

Before sending in my manuscript, I had wrestled with the title. I wanted to call the story "A Gift from Thomas," but I kept telling myself the editors would probably prefer something simpler, so I decided to call it "The Star." I took a deep breath, turned the page, and there, across a layout of a beautiful night sky, were the words, "A Gift from Thomas." Tears of joy slid down my cheeks as I realized the editor had discarded my make-do title and given my tribute the very title I had envisioned. And that wasn't all. I couldn't help wondering, *Is it just a coincidence that this magazine has arrived today— November eighth—Thomas' birthday?*

Earlier that day, I had ordered a dozen balloons from a local gift shop. I decided that instead of taking flowers to the cemetery for Thomas' birthday, I would take colorful balloons, release them, and watch them until they were out of sight, sending a birthday message of love heavenward to Thomas.

What had already transpired that day was extraordinary enough, and I almost felt guilty asking for more. But, on my way to pick up the balloons, I found myself praying for one more little sign. "Lord, let me know somehow that Thomas has been part of this day."

As the clerk handed me the colorful mass of balloons, she hesitated. "Would you like another dozen balloons to go with those?" she asked. "I made a mistake on an order earlier. So if you want these, I'd like for you to have them." Then, before I could reply, she added, "And you know, I also have this giant Happy Birthday balloon. You are welcome to that one too if it's a birthday you're celebrating."

I thanked her and walked out of the store virtually covered with balloons. The significance of what had just happened didn't occur to me until I was well on my way to the cemetery. "How many balloons do you have?" whispered a still, small voice.

I did a quick count. I ordered a dozen and the clerk gave me another dozen, that was twenty-four and then the Happy Birthday balloon made twenty-five.

"And how old is Thomas today?" the voice prodded.

"Twenty-five," I whispered.

Once again, God had heard the cries of a mother's heart. A day filled with loss and disappointment became a day of rejoicing and celebration as I envisioned Thomas standing with the Creator of all birthdays, smiling, and waiting for twenty-five balloons to make their journey across Heaven's gates.

I got out of the car at the cemetery, gathered the balloons from the back seat, and walked to the spot where I would set them free. One by one, I let them go. Compared to the vastness of Heaven, I felt small as I watched the kaleidoscope of colors dance upward into the blue sky. I waited to send the last and biggest balloon—the huge silver Happy Birthday balloon. I hugged it tight, kissed it, and released it to deliver my celebration of love to Thomas.

As the silver message faded from sight, I realized that there is no distance between Heaven and hearts. I'd touched Heaven and held its splendor in my hands. Celebrating life, both here and there, we exchanged gifts . . . gifts with wings.

Every good and perfect gift is from above,
coming down from the Father of the heavenly lights,
who does not change like shifting shadows.
James 1:17

Chicken Nugget

From
High Flight
by John Gillespie Magee, Jr.
(1922-1941)

Oh! I have slipped the surly bonds of earth

And danced the skies on laughter-silvered wings:

Sunward I've climbed, and joined the tumbling mirth

Of sun-split clouds—and done a hundred things

Up, up the long, delirious, burning blue

I've topped the wind-swept heights with easy grace

Where never lark or even eagle flew—

And, while with silent lifting mind I've trod

The high untresspassed sanctity of space,

Put out my hand and touched the face of God.

CHAPTER 22

Chicken Hearts and Chocolate Kisses

by Becky Freeman

Valentine's Day! What a wonderful, lovey-dovey time of year. Time for heart-shaped boxes filled with luscious chocolates that turn women's bodies into heart-shaped balloons. Time for pink teddy bears, long-stemmed roses, love letters, and romantic cards. It can be enough to make everyone a little queasy.

I'll never forget the card Scott gave me on our first "married" Valentine's Day. It would have been lovely, sentimental, and touching, except that he signed it, "Love, Scott Freeman."

As a young bride of seventeen, I was crushed. *How could Scott make a joke of this, our first Valentine's Day as man and wife?* As a young groom of eighteen, Scott was equally mortified. *How in the world could I have messed up so badly, accidentally signing my first and last name?* he thought. Unfortunately, it would not be the last Valentine's Day that ended with two of us sleeping back to back in silence.

As a matter of fact, Scott and I lived in sheer terror of all special occasions for many long years. It is hard to confess this because so much joy and warmth and *specialness* are supposed to begin bubbling up around birthdays, anniversaries, Christmas,

Thanksgiving, Valentine's Day, and such. You name a holiday, and I guarantee we've blown it to smithereens at least once in our twenty-three years of marriage. Even obscure celebrations are susceptible. We've had spats on Groundhog's Day, for goodness sake. One year, there was even a very iffy Daylight Saving's Day. It doesn't take much of a calendar event to turn us into two walking nervous ticks.

Ironically, we are fairly jolly souls on regular days. We only turn into grumps on days when we are expected to be especially cheerful. The added pressure for all to be calm and all to be bright just seems to push us over the edge. Worst of all, special days are the romantic ones, when we are *supposed* to feel like sweethearts joined at the lips. We would have been wise to take a few lessons from a seven-year-old.

A few years ago, our youngest child, Gabe, was struck full force with one of Cupid's arrows. I mean the arrow hit him straight in the heart. One day around mid-February, I happened upon a couple of notes Gabe had penned to his new little love. Its heartfelt sincerity was palpable:

Deer Valentim

I love you more than dimmines. Yur more preshus than baby Jesus lyin in a manjer with sheperds watching over.

love, Gabe

P.S. its all true

Gabe decided to give his new girl the best present his savings could buy. So he gathered up all his dollars, quarters, dimes, and pennies and bought a big fluffy white teddy bear. His sweetheart loved it and wrote to tell him so. Gabe was so touched that he wrote her the following note, which I found a few days later typed on the computer:

Deer Valentim

I'm glad you liked yur teddey bear. I rote a rime for you and it goe'es like this

I think yur grandey

I think yur handey & I like to give candey.

It's short but you know I love you & that's all that matter's.

love, Gabe

Oh, for the heart of a child. After a few years and a little rejection, we grown-ups learn to temper our loving emotions by growing more cautious about wearing our hearts on our sleeves. But not so with kids.

That special Valentine's year, Gabe also came home with a folder stuffed with school worksheets, coloring pages, dime-store cards, and boxes of hard candy hearts with deep, meaningful messages on them like, "Be mine." There among the papers, I found yet another gem. Apparently Gabe's teacher had given the class a special Valentine's Day assignment and Gabe, in his matter-of-fact manner, complied with the following:

I'm polst to tell you good things about Valentims. They are giving presents becouse it's fun to watch them open it. I usually give my friends stufft bears & chocklets. The partys are fun becouse we get cookies, candy, pop, & I can be with my friends. I just flat out like Valentims.

I can't help myself. It's "just flat out" hard not to smile when you've got a sugar-lovin', tenderhearted kid around the house to remind you that love and special days are supposed to be simple and fun. If Scott and I had kept our childlike hearts, we might have "just flat out liked Valentims, too."

Unfortunately, we thought growing up meant turning something sweet and precious into an elaborate ordeal.

Though I must be honest and report that holidays are still a bit touch and go with us, Scott and I have learned some lessons over the years. We've adjusted our expectations of the "perfect romantic day." We try to enjoy whatever comes our way and not to take ourselves too seriously.

As I contemplate some of the successful celebrations we've shared over the years, the one I look back on with particular fondness is our fifth anniversary. Zach was just a baby, and Zeke was, as we say here in the South, "in the oven." We couldn't afford a baby-sitter, but we scraped enough change together to split a barbecue dinner and a large Coca-Cola™, with enough left over to see a movie. The movie, as I recall, was about a young married couple from Texas who had a hard time getting along, though they loved each other deeply. The theme seemed vaguely familiar.

I also remember that Scott and I wore faded jeans and plaid shirts, my hair hung in two Indian-style braids. We sat at the back of the theater, cross-legged in the seats, eating popcorn and taking turns bouncing Zachary to sleep. The pressure to be "the perfect couple having the perfect romantic experience" had been released earlier in the day—the moment we realized we were broke with no babysitter. Yet we were both surprised with how good and how right this simple evening turned out to be.

As I glanced toward Scott in the darkened theater, I felt a tenderness I still recall with a smile. I leaned close to my young husband—with Zachary now asleep on his knee—then thoughtfully rubbed my tummy, where new life was kicking up a storm. Without grandiose expectations, there was no nervousness, no pressure—just a sweet, relaxed evening together as man and wife (and babies).

One of the great surprises of my life has been how it is these simple moments, accumulated over time, that give confidence to a union. A kiss on the cheek. A radio song dedicated to the one you love. A quick neck rub. Gifts, dates, expressions of love don't have to be complicated, expensive, or lengthy. A two-line poem from the heart is better than a long, fancy sonnet written only to impress. As a matter of fact, I'd like to share a closing heartfelt poem dedicated to you, our beloved readers:

May your day be special, filled with love

Simple and sweet from the Father above.

As a wise kid once said, "It's short, but you know I love you—and that's all that matters."

There is no fear in love.
1 John 4:18

Chicken Nugget

From
Redneck Ode to Valentine's
(Author Unknown)

Me n' you's like a Moon Pie™
With an RC™ cold drank,
We go together
Like a skunk goes with stank.

Some men, they buy chocolate
For Valentine's Day
They git it at Wal-Mart,
It's romantic that way.

Some men git a rose
On that special day
From the cooler at Kroger
"That's impressive," I say.

Some men buy fine diamonds
From a flea market booth.
"Diamonds are forever,"
They explain, suave and couth.

But for this man, honey,
These will not do.
For you are too special,
You sweet thang you.

I got you a gift,
Without taste nor order,
Better than diamonds
It's a new trollin' motor.

CHAPTER 23

A Feather in His Cap

by Fran Caffey Sandin

As Steve packed his belongings he said, "Mom, I feel like a soldier prepared for battle and I'm ready to go to war."

I heard his words, but my stomach churned at the thought of our firstborn leaving the nest. With tender emotions, we shuttled our boy to College Station, Texas, where he began adjusting. Ready to try his wings, he flew from a high school class of eight to roost with 11,000 freshmen in the eighth largest university in the United States.

Unlike the other students, Steve had an extra hurdle to jump. He was one of the first graduates of Greenville Christian School. When a Christian school opened in our area, we transferred our children immediately, throwing in our support even before the school earned accreditation. Steve received an unconditional acceptance to Texas Tech, but he wanted to attend Texas A&M, which required students from nonaccredited high schools to enter as summer provisional students. Steve would have to prove that he could do the work before he would receive a green light to continue.

Steve made A's and B's on everything except algebra, a fast-paced course that stretched him to the limit. Unless he passed the course, he would not be allowed to stay at Texas A&M. On the morning of his final algebra exam, I prayed, "Lord, please help him work the problems."

Later that week when I went to pick him up for semester break, he met me at the door with a big smile. "Mom, I made it! I needed 450 total points," Steve explained. "I had 331 going into the test and I made 119 on the exam."

Wow! Exactly the amount he needed. No more, no less. God answered our prayers, and Steve not only continued at A&M but went on to greatness. (The following semester, he made an "A" in calculus—yeah!)

After a couple of years, Steve decided to become a physical therapist. Jim and I encouraged him. His qualities of patience, gentleness, and determination would be an asset in the profession. As a college junior, he applied for the first time to Southwestern Medical in Dallas. He became an alternate candidate for the class, but was not called. In 1992, he graduated from Texas A&M with a degree in kinesiology. We thought surely this time he would succeed. Again we were disappointed. The applicant pool had ballooned to 750 students for 30 class openings, and Steve didn't even receive an interview.

Steve persevered and continued submitting applications until he won an interview at another Texas school. While waiting on an alternate list, he worked at a sports medicine clinic in Fort Worth. The school year started, but no call came. Another disappointment.

A year later, Steve moved to Albuquerque, New Mexico, where he attended the University, took some post-graduate courses, worked in a health club, and continued to apply to physical therapy schools across the country. He flew to Pittsburgh, Pennsylvania, for an interview, but was not chosen. In 1994, Steve returned to Fort Worth and worked in a finance company. They offered him managerial training, but Steve elected not to give up his pursuit of physical therapy.

Jim and I prayed that Steve would not lose heart, but it seemed every door he tried slammed in his face. Most of the rejections occurred around Christmas. We often struggled with discouragement during the holidays. Yet Steve found supportive friends and attended Bible studies wherever he lived.

One morning, I read the Scripture: "For the earth will be full of the knowledge of the LORD as the waters cover the sea" (Isaiah 11:9). Somehow the words, "as the waters cover the sea" seemed significant, but at the time I didn't know why.

That year Kirby Horton, a local therapist, informed Steve of a new school located in St. Augustine, Florida. The Institute of Physical Therapy had an outstanding reputation. Steve applied. Again, we waited.

Every evening before we fell asleep for the night, Jim and I would join hands and pray for Steve. "Our son has worked so hard and had so many disappointments, Lord. Please open the door for him this time."

We were ecstatic when Steve was granted his interview and flew off to Florida with high hopes. We were even more thrilled when he called to say, "Mom and Dad, the school is great! And guess what? It's about two miles from the ocean and a wonderful beach."

From the ocean? From the sea? Was this the promise God gave to me? The entire family waited anxiously to learn whether Steve would be accepted. "After fifteen rejects," he confided, "if this door doesn't open, I'll be looking to another career." Although difficult to part with a dream, Jim and I supported his decision.

In God's waiting room, I alternated between fear, worry, and jubilation. Sometimes I'd be thanking God—on other days I would be crying anxious tears. Like the protective mother hen that I am, I would pray, "Oh, please, Lord, please reward the desire of Steve's heart." As we waited, I found other Bible verses that stilled my fluttering wings. Verses like, "Do not fear or be dismayed . . . for the battle is not yours but God's" (2 Chronicles 20:15 NASB). As God's words calmed my heart, I felt a certainty that God had a wonderful plan for Steve's life.

Then it happened. One autumn evening, the long-awaited answer came. I will never forget his call. "Mom and Dad, I received my letter today. I've been accepted for the class that begins in January!"

Jim and I were thrilled. We screamed, jumped up and down, and hugged each other, but after our celebration was finished, we took hands and thanked God for His answer to our prayers.

Six years after his first application to physical therapy school, Steve gained acceptance into one of the best master's programs in the country. After moving to Florida and spending two tough, hard-working years, Steve completed his studies.

Graduation day, January 14, 1998, in sunny Florida could not have been more beautiful. The organist began playing "Pomp and Circumstance," and I thought we should rename this piece, "Pomp and Overcoming Circumstance." As the visiting professor addressed the class and emphasized the importance of character, we felt so proud of our son. When Steve walked across the stage to receive his diploma, our family stood and cheered. For a moment, I thought I could hear the Lord's applause, too. Steve's smile of satisfaction made an imprint upon my heart. What a glorious, triumphant, memorable ceremony.

Today, as Steve helps rehabilitate a stroke patient or assists an accident victim who must learn to walk again, he can sympathize with the long, grueling process. He has become a caring professional whose cup of courage is full and running over.

For I am confident of this very thing, that
He who began a good work in you will
perfect it until the day of Christ Jesus.
Philippians 1:6 NASB

Chicken Nugget

"God gives every bird its food, but He does not throw it into the nest."
J. G. Holland

CHAPTER 24

Chicken Delight

by Susan Duke

Once a woman we barely knew candidly commented on the fact that my husband and I have very different personalities. "Hon, I bet Harvey helps keep you balanced. You seem so fun-loving and all."

I wasn't sure if I should thank her or feel insulted. "Well, you know, you're probably right. He does keep my feet on the ground . . . and sometimes I let him fly!" A faint but curious smile crossed her face as she walked away. The truth is, she hit a nerve. If a scientific study were done to prove that "opposites attract" Harvey and I would make the perfect test chickens.

He's organized. I'm not. He's a loner. I'm a people person. He thinks I'm too laid back while I often refer to him as "Mr. Intense." When it comes to special occasions, Harvey leans toward practical gift giving. I, on the other hand, (at least in Harvey's opinion) tend to be impractical and a little wild and wacky—going to extremes at times to make a memory. He loves to remind me of the year I almost rented a real chimpanzee for his birthday.

I was determined to make it a birthday Harvey would never forget. He loves to go to the zoo and is especially intrigued with the monkeys. I can't tell you how many times he has remarked that it would be great fun to have a monkey—if you didn't have to deal with all the monkey maintenance. One day I spotted an ad for a chimp in the local paper. Sam, the chimp, and his owner, Stan, were available for birthday parties.

Perfect, I thought, *Harvey's birthday is only a week away.* I picked up the phone and dialed Stan's number.

"Hello, this is Stan. Have I got a deal for you!" the raspy voice chided on the other end of the phone.

"Well, Stan, I certainly hope so. I'm calling about renting your chimpanzee, Sam, as a birthday surprise for my husband. Can you tell me your fee and if Sam can come to a birthday dinner next week?" I asked hopefully.

When I gave him the date, he checked his calendar and responded, "Yeah, yeah, we're available that evening. Give me your address, send me two hundred dollars in advance, and we'll be there in time for supper. We stay for fifteen minutes . . . max."

"Did you say two hundred dollars?" I couldn't hide my shock at such an exorbitant amount. "For only fifteen minutes? And I feed you and Sam a T-bone steak too? Do people actually book you?"

"That's it, lady, take it or leave it," Stan quipped gruffly.

"I'm afraid I'll have to leave it. Thanks anyway."

I was disappointed as I hung up the phone. Oh well, it was a fun thought at least. When Harvey's birthday arrived, I prepared him an extra special steak dinner—without the monkey business—and gave him a funny card that said, "I have good news and bad news." Inside it said, "The good news is . . . I've rented forty dancing girls for your birthday. The bad news is . . . they're all about your age!" Then I told him about almost getting him a dinner date with the chimp of his dreams, but that it was way beyond our already stretched budget. I saw the true meaning of the saying, "It's the thought that counts," when just hearing about the idea brought a huge smile to his face.

Over the years, Harvey's become a little more comfortable with my way-out antics, and we've learned to embrace our differences while keeping an understanding of one thing: that it's not only okay to create special moments in our marriage, it's essential. We have our problems like anyone else (which would take more than one chapter to tell!). But the little things that have given our relationship its own personality have helped us overcome any crisis we've faced.

Soon after we met, Harvey and I gave each other nicknames: "Daddy Bear" and "Baby Bear." Strangely enough, these nicknames have become a common bond that overrides our very different personalities. They've been instrumental in keeping our hearts young toward each other.

I'll never forget our first Christmas, when, on Christmas morning, Harvey awoke to find a giant stuffed teddy bear under the tree with his name on it. He looked like a little boy as he smiled, hugged his bear, and said, " I can't believe you got me— a grown man—a teddy bear, but I love it." From that moment, bears became a standard gift for birthdays, Valentine's Day, and anniversaries. Harvey even puts together an "Easter Bear" basket for me every year.

Although Harvey fills a doorway with his presence and sometimes comes across as serious and abrupt, I know the truth. Underneath, he is a teddy bear with a compassionate heart as big as the sky.

Recently, a close acquaintance shared a concern about her fragile marriage. "My husband and I just don't seem to have anything in common, and we're growing further and further apart. We rarely do anything special or fun. How do you and Harvey keep the spark alive in your marriage?"

"Well, there are lots of simple things that will brighten the dullest relationship. For instance, last year, I suggested to Harvey that we make our own Valentine cards for each other rather than buying them. At first, he wasn't thrilled, but the idea grew on him after awhile. One night shortly before Valentine's, I was surprised when I started into the utility room and found a "No Bears Allowed" sign on the closed door. When the big day finally arrived, I handed him the elegant, Victorian-looking card I had crafted, and he presented me with his two winsome and charming bear cards. Those cards and his written sentiment are among my most priceless treasures.

Thinking back, Harvey has truly been "the wind beneath my chickenhearted wings." When he occasionally accompanies me to a speaking engagement, he ends up unloading the sound system, boxes of tapes and books, and all sorts of things. He's even slung my purse over his shoulder a few times. There are many ways he's offered his love and support of my writing, speaking, and singing.

When I'm pressed for time, he'll cook a meal or help me prepare for company. When he's home and I'm writing, he brings a cup of coffee to my office. And if stay up most of the night, he'll unplug the phone the next morning and let me sleep. When he's in the mood to chill out or rest, I try to be as considerate of him.

Celebrating life's special moments takes time and effort, but it puts the pizzazz and delight in living. When you take the time to create a special moment for your spouse, a friend, a child, or a parent, you've pulled the stopper out of your heart and let all the love inside spill out to another heart.

There are blessings and special moments in our lives, waiting yet to be. But they probably won't just happen. Having the courage to be a little bold, a little daring, even a little childlike, to make sure they happen—on purpose—will bring delight and joy to your life and to others.

Think of it as our way of thanking God and celebrating His precious gift of life.

The LORD your God . . . will take great delight
in you, he will quiet you with his love,
he will rejoice over you with singing.
Zephaniah 3:17

Chicken Nugget

"How good is a man's life, the mere living!
How fit to employ all the heart and soul
and senses forever in joy!"
Robert Browning

CHAPTER 25

Butterball Blessings

by Fran Caffey Sandin

I shivered in the cold wind and pulled my coat further up around my neck. Resting on a flat bed trailer behind my grandfather's old tractor, I noticed the stars seemed brighter than ever in the clear, frigid, spring skies. Ma told me I would freeze if I went with Pa. Now I believed her and wished for my fuzzy flannel nightgown and cozy covers.

The old tractor jerked and groaned as we repeatedly started and stopped. Trying desperately to save a fruit crop threatened by a late freeze, Pa had decided to warm the blossoming trees by placing smudge pots around them. Breathing pungent kerosene fumes and smoke, Pa's helper, Willie, and I rode on the trailer and hopped off at each stop to place the black, flame-tipped pots. I thought we'd never finish.

We returned home very late that evening, and I felt tired and sick. Despite his own fatigue, Pa headed for the kitchen, rattled some dishes, and mixed a fresh, hot lemonade drink for us that warmed me all the way to my toes. When I finally crawled into bed, I felt good. I had helped my Pa.

The next morning Pa prayed, "Lord, give us thankful hearts for these and for all our many blessings." It was the same prayer he prayed over every meal. Pa depended on God for everything, so I knew he meant every word.

Bright sunshine soon replaced the East Texas cold snap. But bad weather at the wrong time had greatly diminished Pa's crop of peaches and plums, a major source of his income. As a grade-schooler living near my grandparents, I carefully observed their responses to various situations. In spite of adversity, Pa seemed to view the bigger picture of life. He worked hard, but like the Apostle Paul, he also seemed content in his circumstances, whatever they might be. He acknowledged God's goodness, and he never missed a day of thanking Him for His blessings.

Long after Pa passed away, I remembered his sweet, humble spirit, and I wanted to recapture his attitude for my own brood. A grateful heart had already become more than just a memory as I tried to personalize Pa's prayer; but prayers of thanksgiving became even more special when I grew up, got married, and had children of my own.

Last year we spent Thanksgiving at the lake house. On that crisp, fall day many trees stood naked, as brightly colored leaves lay in piles around their trunks. A log crackled in the fireplace and the aroma of hot, spiced cider filled the air. It promised to be a perfect day, and I remembered previous years—the children jumping into piles of leaves, swinging in the hammock, and running around with our yellow Labrador; young people enjoying canoeing, volleyball, fishing, or throwing footballs and Frisbees; and as many as twenty-five adults gathered around the cloth-covered ping-pong table catching up on family news, discussing world events, and lingering soulfully over a slice of Mother's deluxe pecan pie.

With visions of sweet potatoes and cranberry relish dancing in my head, I opened the oven, slid in our twenty-four-pound

Butterball™ turkey, and turned the knob on the old lake house oven. It took only a few minutes for me to realize that I was knee deep in turkey feathers. The oven was still as cold as an iceberg. None of my tricks worked. The heating element had warmed its last casserole. With only a few hours to spare before family and special friends were to arrive with side dishes in hand, I called a neighbor.

"Lois," I said with panic in my voice, "everyone will be here in just a few hours and the main course is as cold and clammy as half-thawed fish sticks. HELP!"

Lois just laughed and said, "Honey, bless your little heart. You bundle that turkey up and bring it to my house. We'll have it cookin' in no time."

"Thanks so much. I'll be right over," I squawked, giddy with relief.

I grabbed the turkey-filled roaster pan, loaded it into the car, and drove across the road. My vivacious friend, Lois, babysat the big bird while I returned to the lake house and prepared a festive table. With the turkey cooked to perfection in her oven, I gave special thanks for gracious neighbors as well.

As our family members began to arrive, we embraced our precious new granddaughter, Emily Grace, and welcomed two new nephews by marriage. We also paused to remember those who had moved on to their heavenly homes. The circle dwindles and then it grows as the days of our lives move ever forward.

As is our custom, we paused before our meal, stood in a circle, and prayed—farmers, mechanics, electricians, school-teachers, homemakers, nurses, physicians, to name just a few—all joined together in a bond of love for family and for God. Some people mentioned things for which they were particularly thankful and others stood in respectful silence. As inevitably happens, some members of our sentimental bunch began to cry—a tribute to joy rather than sorrow. And then the rest of us joined in until our beaks were red and a box of tissues had made its dutiful trip around the circle.

When the Thanksgiving celebration had ended and the last crumb was swept off the table, I took a deep breath. When everything is going well, being thankful is easy for me. But sometimes it takes extra courage to give thanks—like when I am grieving, when I fail, when a tragedy strikes someone I love, or even when something unforeseen (like a broken-down oven) disrupts my plans. Then being thankful becomes a decision that helps me focus upon God's greatness and not just upon my present circumstances. Thankfulness becomes a great antidote for anxiety. I once heard singer Joann Shelton say, "Praise moves me from Complaint Avenue to Thanksgiving Boulevard."

It's those times when I stop to reflect upon my Pa and the many times I heard him say, "Lord, give us thankful hearts for these and for all our many blessings." I want that to be my prayer, too.

It is good to give thanks to the LORD,
And to sing praises to Thy name, O Most High;
To declare Thy lovingkindness in the morning,
And Thy faithfulness by night.
Psalm 92:1,2 NASB

Chicken Nugget

From
Count Your Blessings
Hymn by Johnson Oatman Jr.
(1856-1922)

Are you ever burdened with a load of care?
Does the cross seem heavy you are called to bear?
Count your many blessings, every doubt will fly,
And you will be singing as the days go by.
Count your blessings, name them one by one;
Count your blessings, see what God hath done;
Count your blessings, name them one by one;
Count your many blessings, see what God hath done.

SECTION IV

Winging It One Day at a Time

Courage When Facing a Crisis—Big or Small

CHAPTER 26

Tucking a Puppy under My Wings

by Becky Freeman

This Christmas I asked my husband and kids and God and—just to be on the safe side—Santa Claus at the mall for a puppy. Now that my own children were growing up, this mother hen needed something to nurture. So I wanted a puppy with all my heart, a little miniature dachshund—like Porshe, Gracie's wiener dog.

Porshe and I have had a great thing going for years. When I visit Gracie's house, she brings me her tennis ball; I throw it on the carpet, and then she brings it back to me. We do this about seven hundred more times, until I finally grow tired of the game. Then she places the ball near my thigh and pushes it with her nose until I am unwittingly sitting on it. I have to admire her persistence.

Porshe snuggles with me contentedly as I sit in the big chair by Gracie's fireplace, sipping hot coffee and editing manuscripts, during our monthly Hens with Pens meetings. There is just something sweet and warm and inspiring about a little dauchsy snoring in my lap.

And when it's time for lunch, Porshe, I must admit, reminds me a bit of myself. She enjoys eating out in a variety of places. So she takes one piece of dog food at a time from her bowl in the kitchen and carries it off to another room to eat it. Then it's back to the bowl for another take-out piece of dog food and then to another room with a more interesting view. I understand this unique aspect of Porshe's personality and was convinced that I needed a little wiener puppy to call my own. So I began to make my Christmas wish known far and wide.

When Christmas Eve arrived, I felt the excitement I used to feel as a small child, anticipating the morning's gifts. Soon I was sure I'd be hugging my own precious poochy. Well, Christmas morning dawned bright and beautiful and when the whole family had assembled, sitting anxiously beneath the tree, my husband and kids, in a great show of pride, presented me with . . . a doggie bed—an empty doggie bed.

"Thank you," I squealed, certain that a cute little pooch would be popping out of the wrapping at any moment. "Surely there's got to be a dog in here somewhere." But alas, there was no bundle of fur. No cute, whimpering puppy noises.

"Becky," Scott said in quick explanation, "I found a place to get you a puppy, a good healthy puppy. But it won't be born for about six more weeks. Then it will be six weeks after that before it's ready to be taken from its mother. But I've heard with miniature dachshunds that it is important to get a dog of great quality."

I smiled, but I'm sure the disappointment must have shown on my face. Twelve weeks before I got to hold my own puppy? *I didn't care if I had a "dog of great quality," I just wanted a puppy on Christmas Day. Was that too much to ask?*

The next morning, as I sat at the computer typing away on an assignment, I looked up to see my husband, my hero, standing in the doorway holding a wriggling black puppy. I could barely speak as I held out my arms for the bundle of fluff. She was perfect in every way, and I quickly named her Sweet Pea.

"I couldn't stand it," said Scott. "You looked so disappointed." The wriggly wienie dog slid down from my lap and galloped her clumsy way toward my husband. He reached down to pet her as she playfully licked his hand.

"See," I said, beaming with pride. "I told you. She's absolutely perfect."

And she was! Sweet Pea slept all night without a murmur and mostly, went potty outside on the grass. She snuggled with me and the kids as we went about our work. I would often tuck her into my pocket where she'd sleep as I swept and walked and washed dishes. In the evenings, we'd let her chase gift bows and plastic balls until we were all laughing at her wobbly antics. And then, the kids and I would put a furry Christmas stocking cap on her head to keep her extra warm before tucking her into the soft doggie bed.

I was totally enamored by this new life, this bit of baby dog. On New Year's Eve my parents even came over to have their first peek at "the granddog" and left plenty impressed. My mother smiled as she rocked Sweet Pea to sleep, all snug in her Christmas stocking.

It was only two days later that disaster struck. The little puppy who had so completely stolen our hearts stopped eating. Later in the evening, she began to shiver, and I held her close in the crook of my neck all night long to keep her tiny body warm until I could get her to the vet the next morning.

By morning Sweet Pea was worse; nothing stayed down in her tiny belly. We could see the outline of her ribs, and she no longer wanted to move, much less frolic and play. She'd let me hold her but whimpered pitifully every time I shifted or moved.

As soon as the sun came up, I drove our sick little puppy to the animal clinic. The veterinarian took one look at her and said sadly, "Becky, it looks like Parvo." Even though I had no idea what Parvo was, it wasn't difficult to understand that it was serious, probably even fatal.

"We'll do what we can," the vet promised. "We'll start her on IV's and keep her as comfortable as possible. The cost will be high—$150.00 to keep her overnight and each day it will be at least $50.00 to $100.00 more."

I winced at the price, but what could I say? She was my Sweet Pea; I had to try to save her. I nodded to the vet, gave Sweet Pea a gentle snuggle, and then tried to see my way out of the office door to the parking lot through a haze of tears. In seven days I'd gone from anticipation to disappointment, to elation, and now this terrible sadness.

I went home to cocoon, trying not to glance toward the empty dog bed or the red fur-lined stocking cap. I e-mailed all my friends in high places and low places and asked them to pray for my puppy, if their theology would allow such a thing.

The next morning the vet's assistant called with bad news. "Becky, I'm so sorry. Sweet Pea didn't make it through the night." I cried as though I'd lost a good friend, and indeed, I felt that I had. I dreaded telling my daughter, Rachel, who had kept Sweet Pea in her room and cared for her like a little mommy. It's amazing to me how such a tiny ball of fluff could provoke such feelings of love and loss.

The day after Sweet Pea died, I woke up with shooting pains going up my neck and into the top of my head—a crick—from snuggling Sweet Pea on the night she was so sick. *It'll go away soon,* I thought to myself as I rubbed the tender muscles.

It has now been a full month since we lost our puppy and though my neck is still sore, my heart is beginning to heal. Today I tucked away Sweet Pea's dog bed for safekeeping. In a little more time, as soon as I'm well—neck and soul—I plan to be a mother hen to another wobbly, snuggly, baby puppy. And yes, the worst might happen, *could happen* again. Baby animals are short on lifetime guarantees.

I regret neither the pleasure nor the pain of having loved our little Sweet Pea. To refuse the pain would be to diminish the love; and love, as much as it hurts sometimes, is the stuff that makes life worth living.

It takes courage to risk caring. . . .

But that's a risk love has to take.

There is no fear in love.
But perfect love drives out fear.
1 John 4:18

Chicken Nugget

"The great pleasure of a dog is that you may make a fool of yourself with him and not only will he not scold you, but he will make a fool of himself, too."

Samuel Butler

CHAPTER 27

Too Pooped to Cluck

by Rebecca Barlow Jordan

"Where do you hurt?" The clean-cut orthopedist raised his miniature tape recorder to his mouth and mumbled something into it before I could respond.

I sniffed the antiseptic air and cleared my throat, not knowing if this was a live radio interview or a case study for the *Scientific Journal of Medicine*. Any minute, I expected to see a skylight open up overhead and a half dozen white-coated interns pop into view to observe some experimental procedure.

"All over—more than anywhere else," I quipped, in answer to his question.

His expression never changed—definitely not a "Patch Adams" personality. So I rambled on. "I wake up all hours of the night; my back hurts, and when my husband squeezes my arms or calf muscles playfully, I wince with pain—and I tire easily. Where has my strength gone?"

He ignored my complaints, and instead, asked me to try a few basic exercises. "Hmmm," said the young man into the black box, as he began a droning monologue. "Patient is tall and thin—cannot touch her toes, comes within three inches of the floor."

After firing a barrage of questions at me, he seemed satisfied with my answers. I was eager for a quick fix—a pill, a shot, some RX to heal the problem. But it wasn't that easy. I heard a click that silenced the whirring of the small recorder. The orthopedist grew quiet and thoughtful. "I think you have fibromyalgia," he concluded.

"Fibromy-what?" I said innocently. It sounded like something growing in my backyard birdbath.

He tried to explain in layman's terms, but that can be an almost impossible feat for some medical professionals. When I left his office, the only two phrases I remembered were, "no cure," and "gentle and moderate exercise for life." I named the things I would have to relinquish: *No more dashes down icy slopes!* I thought. And I did love skiing. The one time I flew down the slopes without falling was pure poultry in motion. No more bowling—not a great loss. The last time I had tried that, Larry spent two days trying to pry my aching body out of bed. Now I understood why.

Although I didn't know it at the time, I had become a common statistic. According to the American College of Rheumatology, of the 34,000,000 people in America who suffer with chronic pain, three to six million have fibromyalgia syndrome. I would soon learn that recurrent pain, in one form or another, sneaks into our lives like a fox in a henhouse. Slowly, subtly it tiptoes through our bodies, wreaking havoc and stealing strength, leaving behind emotional, physical, or even spiritual distress—pain that can often immobilize otherwise healthy lives.

In the first few years after my diagnosis, I felt like my grandmother's pincushion. One physician constantly ordered blood tests to see if his prescribed medications were causing other problems. They did. When every prescription made my liver quiver, I cried, "Enough!" Finally, one doctor who did help relieve my irregular sleeping patterns with a mild prescription, explained part of the problem in a language I could understand: "Because the muscles party all night, you don't get enough rest. Sleep and exercise are two keys you can't do without."

Like all patients with chronic pain, I faced a choice. I had far exceeded the Apostle Paul's three urgent pleas for healing. And though I continued to pray and believe, like Paul, I seemed to hear God's voice saying, "My grace is sufficient for you. My strength is made perfect in weakness."

One morning I was trying to decide whether to unscramble my cramped muscles and crawl out of my warm waterbed, or stay nestled in for a few more hours. I began to think of others who apparently had learned pain management: Alma, riveted with arthritis, never hesitated to thrust her twisted fingers into a warm handshake, a gesture that complimented her twinkling eyes and radiant glow. An astute Bible teacher, she chose to minister in the midst of her pain.

My friend, Nancy, whose life has been riddled with emotional losses as well as physical pain, stirs the waters of her therapeutic hot tub daily. But after each dip, she always seems to come up smiling—and serving.

I remembered reading about Reverend Ronald Austin, a preacher who stopped for a hitchhiker. Stabbed, entangled in his seat belt, and dragged by a speeding car, he was forced to endure the amputation of his foot. His words upon returning to the pulpit? "I have one leg! Thank You, God!"

My discomfort sometimes appears small, in light of the excruciating pain of these and others—like another friend, Linda, who spends every moment just trying to survive her mysterious illness. But to one who is hurting, pain is pain. The sting of abuse and the throes of sorrow, the anguish of rejection and depression, or even the confusion of spiritual struggles all involve additional chronic pain that is real.

Prayer and counseling, with time, can help heal emotional pain and spiritual dryness. But those with chronic physical pain may think God has forgotten.

Dr. Billy Graham says, "The hurts of today can be the joys of tomorrow." In each of the lives mentioned above, I observed one common denominator: joy. *Of course,* I thought, *if I must have chronic pain—why not choose chronic joy as well?* Chronic—that which reappears again and again. *Yes!*

Not only could I choose chronic contentment and joy, but I would do everything I could to tone my body, mind, and spirit. With God's help, I would try to shape up these rebellious muscles and uncooperative tissues. I began a regiment of mild aerobic exercise, including walking, that would make Richard Simmons proud. I continued a healthy diet and learned to pace my schedule and energy accordingly. Nine years have passed since my first diagnosis. I feel better, most of the time—but I'm saving money for that hot tub.

I would love to see my doctor stamp "Healed" on my records, like he did recently for another physical problem of mine. And God may bring that healing. But that hasn't happened yet.

I have learned to treat myself gently when my pain management grade drops below "A." God doesn't require us to deny our struggles. In the book of Psalms, David asks the Lord to record his tears in a bottle. God cares about our pain. He only wants to change our focus from inward to outward and upward. I am content, knowing that He is always working to make me more like Himself.

Before I underwent a recent surgical procedure, my husband asked me, "Are you concerned . . . fearful?"

"It's not pain I fear the most—or the outcome," I replied. "I guess I'm afraid that somehow I won't honor the Lord through the painful process." Sometimes I fall back into complaining about a lack of energy, to which my own daughter responds, "Mom, you already fill your calendar and every waking moment. What would you do with *more* energy?"

That's when I know it's time to grab my Bible, fluff up my feathered pillow, and head for the backyard hammock again, ready for another of God's lessons on "joy management."

For our light and momentary troubles are achieving for us
an eternal glory that far outweighs them all.
2 Corinthians 4:17

Coping with Fibromyalgia Syndrome

Chicken Nugget

1. Work carefully with a doctor who can help treat your unique symptoms.

2. Avoid or try to reduce stress. Allow time to relax and do things you enjoy.

3. Start a program of mild exercise, building to twenty to thirty minutes four times a week.

4. Get plenty of sleep. Some doctors prescribe a non-addictive antidepressant to help.

5. Meditate on God's Word daily, and focus on positive thoughts.

6. Although chronic pain is no laughing matter, laughter is good medicine.

7. Try a good back pillow, massage, hot bath, and daily Icy Hot™ rub-downs.

8. Enlist the support of family and friends who understand.

9. Find ways you can still minister to others through your own particular gifts.

10. Eat a healthy diet and drink at least eight glasses of water each day.

CHAPTER 28

What's in Your Coop?

by Becky Freeman

I followed my husband out to his car to give him a kiss before he drove off to work. As I started to reach my arms around his neck, I had to stop and laugh instead. "Scott, what is all this stuff you're carrying?"

"I can explain," he said thoughtfully. "See, I'm taking the Beanie Baby™ lion to put in my office—to go with the other ones you've given me. This is my mug of coffee, and the taco chip—well, that's my breakfast."

"I suppose that bottle of vitamins is to counteract the effect of the coffee and corn chip breakfast?" I asked with a grin.

"You got it."

"And the tape measure?"

"Hey, you never know when you might need one. A man's always gotta have a tape measure—a pocket knife and tape measure." I gave him a curious look. "It's a man thing, Becky. Just think of it as a guy's form of lipstick and powder."

Off and on throughout the morning, I thought about what Scott held in his hands, how it reflected parts of his personality. The taco chip and vitamin bottle were perfect representations of the battle he wages between wanting to be healthy and loving quick junk food. The macho "Construction Guy" measuring tape contrasted with the "Little Boy" soft, stuffed animal. Two contrasting sides of his man/boy personality.

Then I began thinking about all the crazy things we humans pack in our hands, our purses, our backpacks, our personal spaces—and even on the backs of our vehicles. As I drove to town that afternoon, I stopped at a light behind a family-looking car, a nice blue Ford Tempo™. But I couldn't help noticing the odd array of bumper stickers. Beside a sticker from "Treasure Chest Tattoos" was a picture of a chubby blue Teddy Bear. Just underneath that interesting arrangement, was a peace symbol and a MADD sticker. Here in Texas—the buckle of the Bible and the gun belt—one is likely to see a bumper sticker that says, "You can have my rifle when you pry my cold dead fingers off of it," pasted right next to "Honk if you love Jesus." A car psychologist would have a field day analyzing our Southern bumpers.

I was at a lady's retreat recently, and we were asked to share the most unusual items in our purses—the oddest offering would receive a prize. What the women in this small church packed in their purses simply amazed me. From their sedate-looking leatherette handbags, they pulled out things like barbed wire cutters; a plastic, unfoldable potty seat cover; an industrial-sized can of disinfectant; and entire boxes of food—crackers, cookies, even a large can of Spaghettios™.

Again I began to think about how the things in our possession say something about who we are and what we want and need. Looking around my office as I write these words, I realize I have feathered my writing nest with a variety of affirming photos and notes, most of them taped to the window above my computer. They serve as visual reminders of love, giving me courage to keep on keeping on when the road ahead gets weary.

There's a photo of me with my original family—mother, daddy, brother, and sister snuggled on a couch. A note from my sister, Rachel, during a particularly tough period of dealing with writing disappointments. She'd paraphrased a country song for me: "Write like you don't need the money, love like you'll never get hurt, dance like nobody's watching, Beck. It has to come from the heart if you want it to work."

There's a photo of my youngest son, Gabe, sleepily hugging my neck and a note from my oldest son, Zach, starting out with the line, "A standing ovation for the best parents a young man could ever have. . . ." (I re-read that a dozen times after one particularly bad mother-son argument.) There are twinkie-style pictures of me and my daughter in big floppy straw hats and a picture of my son, Zeke, in his football uniform—wearing sunshades.

One of my favorite photos is of me sitting on Scott's lap on a recent anniversary. Below it is a romantic note from him saying, "A man could have no greater blessing than to have the love of a woman like you." (I stare at that photo on days when matrimony doesn't feel quite so merry.)

There's a big handwritten page of the Love Chapter from 1 Corinthians 13 TLB to remind me over and over again: "Love is very patient and kind . . . never haughty or selfish or rude. . . ." And there's a poster of bright purple sheep that I love, with the caption: "I was normal once, I didn't like it."

In the midst of the dried-out markers and empty cups of day-old coffee, there's a verse my mother-in-law wrote on a card several years ago. She slipped it into my hand before I spoke in front of a large audience. The card said simply, "Psalm 27:1 KJV '. . . the Lord is the strength of my life; of whom shall I be afraid?'"

I keep a handwritten note from dear friend and mentor, Bob Briner, tacked to the window. "Becky—from honorary doctorates,

Emmys, and Aces, a number of citations have come my way, but none are more cherished than your comments about me in your book." It reminds me of the power a word of simple praise and appreciation can have in another person's life.

In a small white frame is a note signed by Erma Bombeck, a role model in humor, in response to a letter I wrote her as she was suffering from kidney disease. In essence, I've surrounded myself with cheerleaders—in pictorial and written form.

How comforting it was to hear that even Abraham Lincoln needed tangible encouragement to spur his sometimes sagging confidence. When Lincoln was tragically killed, several items were found in his pockets: an embroidered handkerchief, a watch, and some confederate money. But most interesting of all was a ragged copy of a newspaper article. The article had been written during a time of great controversy and turmoil in the country. In the text of the article, the writer extolled Lincoln's virtues, approving of the decisions he had made in office. What a poignant thought—even one of our greatest presidents needed a note of praise in his pocket, where it could be easily found in moments of doubt and despair.

The truth is there's not a human being alive who doesn't need a little dose of affirmation now and then. So along with the crazy things we humans pack in our pockets and purses and Pontiacs, along with the half-eaten sandwiches and wire cutters, we need to be sure and tuck in some encouragement for our journey through this life.

If you are feeling especially henpecked or puny or just plain chicken this week, be on the lookout for some healthy feed to put in your pocket. Perhaps one of the following P's: a poem, a prayer, a promise, or a praise. Then read those uplifting words whenever your feathers are wilting. In no time, you'll be fluffed up and crowing again.

Let not mercy and truth forsake you; bind them around
your neck, write them on the tablet of your heart.
Proverbs 3:3 NKJV

Presidential Points to Ponder & Pack

Chicken Nugget

"Do not worry, eat three square meals a day, say your prayers, be courteous to your creditors, exercise, go slow, and go easy. These, I reckon, will give you a good life."

Abraham Lincoln

"When written in Chinese, the word 'crisis' is composed of two characters. One represents danger and the other represents opportunity."

John F. Kennedy

"The older I get, the more wisdom I find in the ancient rule of taking first things first—a process which often reduces the most complex human problems to manageable proportions."

Dwight D. Eisenhower

"Far better it is to dare mighty things, to win glorious triumphs, even though checkered by failure, than to take rank with those poor spirits who neither enjoy much nor suffer much, because they live in the gray twilight that knows not victory nor defeat."

Theodore Roosevelt

CHAPTER 29

One Quick Chick

by Fran Caffey Sandin

I sniffed the new car fragrance and thought—*dependable transportation at last!* As Jim drove our shiny, green station wagon home from the dealership, I smiled with confidence. This will be so great for field trips and ball games. It seemed perfect for our family's needs.

But one week later on a sunny afternoon, my jubilation deposited itself on the pavement without so much as a squeak of warning. As I drove Angie to her piano lesson, the car hummed quietly along Greenville's main street. Then as we topped the rise of a small hill, we heard a very loud clunk.

"Mother!" Angie squealed, a horrified expression crossing her face. "What happened?"

"I don't know," I said, glancing quickly in the rearview mirror. That's when I saw it—a huge pile of metal on the pavement behind us.

"Good grief!" I exclaimed. "I think the bottom just fell out of our car!"

"But, Mother," Angie countered, "it's brand new!"

"I know, Honey. I can't imagine what's wrong."

By this time, the car had lost power and we were coasting downhill. We had enough momentum to glide into a gas station on the corner where I hopped out, explained the problem, and asked to make a local call.

Then I phoned the salesman who had sold us the car. "You know that station wagon we bought from you last week?"

"Sure, Mrs. Sandin. I remember."

"Well, the rear end just fell out on Wesley Street. What are YOU going to DO about it?"

"Ma'am, don't worry. I'll send someone right away."

His voice sounded so calm I wondered if he received calls like mine everyday. Within fifteen minutes, Angie and I were sitting in the tow truck cab, chatting with the driver as he hauled our disabled vehicle in for repairs. The dealer provided a loan car. Angie missed her lesson but we finished our afternoon errands.

Later that evening in a family discussion, we joked that our car was probably assembled on a Monday morning by some folks with a hangover. But after a few more incidents, we stopped laughing.

"Mr. Petty," I would whine to the wrecker driver, "my car has broken down again. Can you haul me in one more time?"

Before long, Mr. Petty's wrecker became a welcomed sight. I learned so much car talk, I could have conversed with the colorful radio personalities/car specialists—Click and Clack, the Tappit Brothers. Alternator, generator, carburetor—I spoke the lingo. If only I understood what the words meant.

My car had a mind all its own. When I pressed the gas pedal to the floor, I could count to ten before the car began to move, then it would barely go. When traveling uphill, my passengers began asking if they should get out and push. Then when I finally reached a smooth driving speed and had to slow down and stop, the engine would die.

Some mechanics attributed the problems to the new pollution-saving devices mandated by the government. I didn't care about the cause—I just wanted a car that would stop and go at the right time.

Although my car radio spit out a steady stream of praise songs and sound preaching, not even the sanctified words of men like Chuck Swindoll, James Dobson, and Tony Evans could make my chariot repent.

One ordinary day as I started driving to town, "The Green Hornet" began surging. At first I thought, *Well, maybe this clunker has some pep after all.* But when it kept accelerating faster, faster, and faster, I knew something was wrong. Especially when my foot wasn't even near the gas pedal. I tried to brake to no avail and then realized the accelerator had stuck! Oh great. Now it's *Chitty Chitty Bang Bang,* and we're ready to fly!

Speeding down Highway 34 North toward Greenville, I needed a siren, but since I didn't have one, I remembered a repair shop about two miles ahead on the right. That would be my target. With only a few cars on the road that day, I zoomed past businesses and whizzed over the Interstate 30 bridge. Like a flash, I topped the incline and tried to slow down enough to make the turn. With my motor roaring, I screeched around the corner, whirled up the driveway, and through the broad garage doors. In order to stop, I literally had to turn off the key before I even pulled into the drive. The smell of burning rubber filled the air. My eyes were as big as goose eggs, and all my feathers were sticking straight out.

I expected to hear applause and see a few bows for riding that racehorse to the barn! But the men in the shop just kept working. No one seemed to notice that I'd just completed the wild, wacky, heart-stopping, blue ribbon finish.

A laid-back, mild-mannered attendant sauntered over to my window and drawled, "Are ya havin' a little problem there, Maa'aaam?"

"Little problem?!?" I felt like screaming.

Frankly, I wanted to push the Green Hornet over the edge of a cliff, wash my hands, and go shop for another car. It really disappointed me this time. This simply had to be the last repair!

It was—for awhile. We finally concluded, the potential four-wheeled coffin had to go. We gave it (with red flags and warnings attached) away to a ministry (that had its own mechanic) and bought another car, a reliable one that's still in the family.

However, those frustrating experiences taught me that sometimes my behavior is just like that old Green Hornet. I'm slow to start doing what I know is right. Or at other times, I jump quickly to the wrong conclusion and fly off in the wrong direction. I'm finding the only place of stability and reliability is in the Lord. The psalmist felt the same as he penned, "Some boast in chariots, and some in horses; but we will boast in the name of the LORD, our God" (Psalm 20:7 NASB). A daily visit to God's repair shop helps me focus upon Him.

In Him all things hold together.
Colossians 1:17 NASB

THEE Repair Shop

Broken windshield wipers:
The commandment of the LORD is pure, enlightening the eyes (Psalm 19:8 NASB).

Faulty horn:
Let the words of my mouth and the meditation of my heart be acceptable in Thy sight, O LORD, my rock and my Redeemer (Psalm 19:14 NASB).

Broken headlight:
For Thou dost light my lamp; the LORD my God illumines my darkness (Psalm 18:28 NASB).

Rear end dragging:
He makes my feet like hinds' feet, and sets me upon my high places (Psalm 18:33 NASB).

Corroded battery:
Wash me, and I shall be whiter than snow (Psalm 51:7 NASB).

Rough-running engine:
When my anxious thoughts multiply within me, Thy consolations delight my soul (Psalm 94:19 NASB).

Leaky radiator:
You have seen me tossing and turning through the night. You have collected all my tears and preserved them in your bottle! You have recorded every one in your book (Psalm 56:8 TLB).

Empty tank:
Be filled with the Spirit (Ephesians 5:18 NASB).

CHAPTER 30

When Good Things Happen to Bad Hens

by Fran Caffey Sandin

Skimming along under starlit skies, a light breeze brushed against our cheeks as my husband and I sailed our boat toward the dock. Our family had enjoyed a fantastic July fourth picnic together at our lake cabin. Then later that evening, when everyone had gone and Jim and I had some time alone, we sailed out to enjoy the spectacular fireworks displays along the shoreline.

We'd often been night sailing and found it restful. So quiet—only the splashing sounds of our boat gliding through the water. I felt relaxed, romantic, and reflective as we headed back home. That is, until I heard a motor and noticed a distant light that seemed to be moving closer and closer to us.

Quickly I remembered my safety training, grabbed a flashlight, flipped the switch, and focused the light upward on our full white sail. We expected the boat to veer away, but it kept coming.

"Jim!" I screamed. "Can't that guy see our running lights?" Since motorboats are supposed to yield the right-of-way to sailboats, we expected the driver would change his course. We couldn't change ours. In the light wind, we didn't have enough speed to maneuver out of his way.

"Why can't he see our sails?" I cried, while flashing the light back and forth across the white expanse above us.

Nothing changed. As the sound of the motor increased, my eyes locked onto the oncoming beam. We watched helplessly as the driver ignored our warnings. The motorboat shot toward us like a missile.

"He's not turning." I cried, "He'll hit us!"

My husband, a seasoned sailor, quietly and wisely kept the bow straight ahead—between our bodies and the oncoming boat.

"Hang on!" Jim said firmly. "Here he comes."

Terrified, I gripped the handrail under the seat. My stomach churned as I thought, *This is it!* Then I sent up a prayer-flare without the formalities of "Dear Lord" and "Amen." Like the Apostle Peter when he began to sink, I just prayed—*help!* The deafening sound came first, then the sickening thud.

Flash! Crash! Jerk! The impact caused our boat to heel dramatically to the left.

The jolt sent me sprawling across the cockpit floor. When the violent swings subsided, I pulled myself back on my feet, clung to the edge of the cabin door, and whirled back onto the seat. Surprised to be in the boat and not in the water, I glanced toward the stern and asked, "Jim, are you okay?"

"I managed to hang on," he said with a slight quiver in his voice.

We listened as the motorboat's soft hum circled us and broke the eerie silence. A young man yelled, "Hey y'all, I'm so sorry. Are y'all okay?"

Unnerved and stunned, I sat quietly while Jim responded, "We're alive." He followed up by asking, "Is anyone hurt?"

"Nope," the young man answered. "We're all okay—just have a bad leak in our boat. Gotta go now." He motored slowly toward the shore where his punctured sixteen-foot craft promptly sank.

Later we learned what happened. Six young adults enthusiastically raced out to watch the fireworks just as we were coming into the cove. As its speed increased to twenty-four miles per hour, the boat's bow tilted upward. Unfortunately, the passengers failed to look where they were going. Isn't it ironic that in spite of a huge lake area with plenty of room for both vessels—we collided? Thankfully, only the driver's pride suffered. We could have all become statistics. If Jim had tried to steer us out of the way by turning broadside to the oncoming boat, I hate to imagine what could have happened. His clear thinking saved our lives.

Our twenty-six-foot, fixed-keel sailboat survived with repairable damage. Shaken, bruised, and sore, we made a decision—no more night sailing. Lake Tawakoni is basically a fishing area with only a few sailboats. It probably wasn't wise to assume everyone would know and observe the waterway rules. We thanked God for His protection and became even more acutely aware of God's precious gift to us—the gift of life.

Still, we never know what may happen. Sometimes it takes courage just to get out of bed and start the day. As I began writing about our boating experience, I recalled another incident from several years ago.

One evening I began driving from my parent's East Texas home to Tyler. Since I worked a night shift at the hospital, I took the shortest, most convenient route—a road through the Sabine River bottom.

The familiar hammock-shaped highway hid in the black night. I didn't know that spring rains had caused the river to begin rising over its banks and out into the lowlands. Just as I topped the first rise and began to descend, I saw three men in a pickup truck stopped beside the road. When I slowed to evaluate the wet pavement ahead, the guys whistled. Believing

I was caught between the devil and the deep blue sea, I decided to continue driving.

A few minutes later, I realized the men had tried in vain to get my attention. Water surrounded me. At that time it was only a few inches deep over the highway, but waves trickled steadily across. What should I do? Instinctively, I turned the headlights on low beam and straddled the center white stripe. "Please, Lord," I kept praying aloud, "please get me through."

I thought my wildly beating heart would break my ribs as I progressed slowly but steadily through the dark. I thanked Him for every inch I moved successfully over the two-mile stretch. It almost seemed like someone was sitting on top of my car! The tires remained solidly on the pavement for the entire length of my journey.

Instead of being washed downstream, never to be seen again, I reached the other side! As I drove up the hill, I began singing and praising God, "Thank You, Lord. Thank You!" My feathers were limp, but I composed myself enough to work my hospital shift.

Many times since that horrifying night, my thoughts have played a rerun of the events. I am always reminded afresh of God's faithfulness. His presence never left me.

Bad things happen to good people. When those painful events occur, our Heavenly Father tenderly comforts us with His tailor-made love. But as we plod through the deep waters of everyday living, good things also happen to bad people. Good things like being rescued from a shipwreck or a dangerous flood. At times we make foolish choices and suffer the consequences, but so often His grace covers even our bad decisions.

Our God never changes. Because He sees us to the end of the path, we can trust Him to guide us through all life's unexpected turns and blind corners. That's why we can face each new day (or night) with confidence.

When you pass through the waters, I will be with you;
And through the rivers, they will not overflow you.
Isaiah 43:2 NASB

Chicken Nugget

He's Real to Me
by Perry Tanksley
From *A Gift of Gratitude*
by Perry Tanksley, Allgood Books
(Box 1197, Clinton, Mississippi 39060),
1967, p. 52. Used by permission.

I've never heard His voice
Nor glimpsed His face so wise
Or gripped His nail-torn hand
Or gazed into His eyes.
Yet echoes of His voice
I've heard above the storm
And oft at worship time
I've glimpsed His shadowed form.
His robe I've never touched
Or heard Him call my name,
Yet He's more real to me
Than any friend I claim.

CHAPTER 31

Eggcess Baggage

by Susan Duke

Waiting for the shuttle bus at the airport, I loosened my grip on the gray mass beside me. It felt like two thousand pounds of dead weight in my right hand. My wrist was weak, frozen in a fixed position, and the throbbing pain was becoming almost unbearable. The source of my discomfort? A gigantic, bulging tweed suitcase. I nicknamed it "The Titanic."

Three of my sister hens, Fran, Rebecca, and Gracie, were accompanying me to a Christian writers' conference in Titusville, Florida. I wanted to make sure I had everything I needed for the six days we'd be gone: dressy and casual shoes; navy for my blue suit, red for my pantsuit, black for my banquet dress, green for my skirt ensemble, brown for my casual pants, and cream in case I opted for my neutral outfit. Of course I must have tennis shoes for the beach, my pink house shoes, pink robe and pajamas, my Bible, notebook, prayer journal, pens, camera, makeup, toiletries, hair dryer, and hot rollers. Just normal, everyday stuff.

I should have known early on that cold January morning when we shoved sixteen pieces of luggage into Fran's jeep, we were in for a challenging trip! But nothing could dampen my excitement and anticipation as we departed for the airport to catch our flight to sunny Florida. I was sure the upcoming days of inspiration and motivation would overshadow any minor inconveniences we might encounter along the way.

Upon reaching the airport, however, I quickly began to realize the consequences of overpacking. I didn't know how many luggage transfers there'd be between the parking lot and the baggage check-in. After walking less than a hundred feet, I suddenly realized I was in dire danger of dislocating a shoulder or possibly misaligning one entire side of my body! Though the Titanic came equipped with nifty rolling wheels, I never saw one of them actually roll. A ball and chain attached to my ankle would have been easier to drag through the airport corridors.

At one point, my strength gave out. I could not move another inch. I was stuck, cemented at the wrist, to what felt like a suitcase full of cinder blocks! I was going down with the Titanic!

To make matters worse, when I surveyed the luggage of my fellow hen travelers, I realized Fran's only bag, other than a small carry-on, was not much bigger than my overloaded makeup case!

"Where is your real suitcase, Fran?" I asked.

"This is it." She patted her small bag. "I have everything I need in here."

"You've got to be kidding! There's no way you can have clothes for six days, personal items, shoes, and a dressy outfit for the banquet in that bag!"

But she did.

When we finally arrived at the conference, I was constantly amazed. Fran always looked as if she'd stepped off the cover of *Vogue* magazine. I, on the other hand, felt more like the cover girl for a new magazine called *Vague!* I hadn't the vaguest notion how anyone could pack so light and look so good!

As I lugged the Titanic from the car to the airport, up a flight of stairs at the hotel, back to the airport, and home, I couldn't help missing the other right brained "hen" in our coop, Becky. Where was she when I needed her? I knew if she'd have been along, she'd have a suitcase just as wild as mine, maybe even one tied with a rope or held together with safety pins!

The suitcase I'd admired for its roomy capacity and saved for long trips had become my enemy! I couldn't help reliving the picture of pain on my friends' faces as they each dutifully helped me, over and over again, with the loading and unloading of my albatross. I regretted the inconvenience I'd caused them all and knew I couldn't have made it without them. However, the joint effort it took to handle this massive suitcase made me think about how burdensome are the suitcases we pack in our own lives.

"Lord," I prayed as I collapsed in a chair after the arduous journey, "is there something You're trying to tell me through this?"

His answer did not surprise me. God began to point out all the extra stuff I carry around in my spiritual suitcase—things that weigh me down, like unresolved pain and unforgiveness, needless worry about the future, finding enough hours in the day to meet deadlines, and the fear of failure.

I also realized that lugging eggcess baggage full of pain, anxiety, and fear, puts a strain and a burden on those who try to help me carry my load. Eggcess baggage doesn't just affect me, it affects everyone in my life. Not only will it cause me to stumble, but it could hinder someone else's journey as well.

"It's time to let go of that eggcess baggage," I felt God speak to my heart.

At least half of my gray suitcase's contents turned out to be completely unnecessary. Most of the stuff hauled 1,000 miles from home lay in my suitcase, untouched. The only lasting result of my extra baggage was an aching wrist that hurt for three months!

Today, the Titanic is history—its empty hulk lies somewhere beneath oceans of other useless stuff on my garage floor. But I will always remember the lessons it taught me. Eggcess baggage never serves God's purpose in our lives; it clutters the soul. Our Father is a God of abundance, and His suitcase of grace is filled to overflowing with all that we will ever need in our journey through life.

Let us lay aside every weight, and the sin
which doth so easily beset us, and let us run
with patience the race that is set before us.
Hebrews 12:1 KJV

Chicken Nugget

Life's Journey

Life's journey has its choices,
We can be bound or free.
And what we choose along life's course
Determines our destiny.

If we choose to carry burdens,
And satchels full of pain,
We'll soon be heavy laden
And crippled with disdain.

But if we choose to carry faith,
Sweet victory we will know—
As we march through life courageously,
We'll conquer every foe.

CHAPTER 32

Will the Real Hen Please Stand Up?

by Rebecca Barlow Jordan

As a child, I loved playing dress-up. In one house a secret passageway connected Mom's closet to mine. There, in a make-believe wonderland of her simple possessions, I'd grab a handful of feathery plumed or pillbox hats, a string of pearls, and a Sunday dress or two—and return to my room for a pretend tea party.

Perhaps the process of discovering our own personalities is a bit like trying on hats. Some fit; some don't. But finding which ones really do is not always easy.

Years later as a young adult, it seemed quite harmless to pretend again—this time as part of a planned youth activity. Each of the youth teachers and some of the church staff chose various persona—some simple, some complex—and we hid ourselves among the hundreds of Saturday mall shoppers. The youth, acting as detectives, and armed with a list of names, scrambled to find their suspects in a two-hour period.

Three adults hid themselves in creaky wheelchairs: two as eighty-somethings with gray hair and woolen shawls, and another resembling an emergency room victim. One teacher, dressed in a '50s plaid sport coat and vest, perched behind a newspaper in a shoe store all day. A mother of three could have easily passed as a "punk" rocker.

One young single guy in his best female impersonation drew a few whistles, but failed to fool many of the high school students. Another dressed as a cowboy, two as "mod" '70s teens, and one, creatively, as himself—darting in and out of the store elevators to escape wary eyes. My own husband posed as a custodian in the food court, sweeping and cleaning, but often resting (and snacking) among the shoppers at the tables. (Why didn't I think of that?)

I decided to disguise myself as an expectant mother by tucking a pillow in the waist of my skirt, then covering it with a maternity smock. As I waddled my cumbersome way through the aisles, some of the youth approached me timidly. Afraid to make a mistake, they cautiously questioned any men standing nearby: "Is that your wife?" But others mustered enough courage to ask me, "Do you go to my church?"

I'd like to think my sunglasses gave me away, but it could have been the shifting "baby" or my tilted, blonde wig. Our simple charades had brought a few stares—and a few chuckles from curious shoppers. But eventually, the youth found us all. When the event was over, I decided maybe blondes do have more fun—or at least those with personalities other than my own.

Perhaps it was that harmless experience or the innocent comment of a friend early in our ministry, "You don't look—or act—like a minister's wife," that ultimately led me to several years of serious pretense. In my secret thoughts, I'd watch other apparent one-dimension personalities and wonder, *Why not try on their hats?* I'd envy those pillars of strength in the church—people whose personalities were as steady and constant as a Christmas evergreen. I'd try to copy the class clowns who kept life's squeaky doors oiled with laughter. Or surely, I, too, could be a bold church women's director who knew where she was going—and who was going with her.

Wouldn't I love to minister in a more creative way, cooped up in romantic, lakeside cottages and dream up works of art? At least with these types, there were no surprises. They *seemed* to be singular in purpose and in personality—typical, and often predictable.

But imitating these and other personalities only made me feel like I was part of some "chickengate" deception. One day I resigned my impersonations and prayed, "God, I'm tired of trying to play a part that is not *me*. From this point on, I'll be myself—if You'll just show me who I really am."

As the years passed, with God's help, I found the courage I needed. I had discovered a freeing truth: The majority of us don't fall into clearly defined categories and easy-to-read labels. God gave each of us a combination of just-right ingredients to fulfill His purpose for our lives. None of us are *strangely* created. Instead, the writer of Psalms tells us we are "fearfully and wonderfully made" (Psalm 139:14 KJV).

In my bedroom closet, I now keep a variety of hats—a fun denim one adorned with a Victorian rose, for dispensing hugs and laughing my way through a cluttered office; a Panama-style one for standing comfortably behind a speaker's podium; a floppy, straw hat for gardening, reminding me to keep growing—constantly rooted in God's Word; and a Southern, wide-brimmed one with which I often hole up in my hammock, when my creative pen becomes the microphone of my soul. Anytime I feel like straying from the typical stereotypes associated with my profession, I don't have to pretend or hide out in the "mall" closet. I can grab any one of these coverings and be totally comfortable just being myself.

Just like with Adam and Eve in the Garden of Eden, if God comes walking by, looks my way and asks, "Where are you? Will the real hen please stand up?" Confidently and without hesitation, all four of me will rise.

Surely you desire truth in the inner parts.
Psalm 51:6

Chicken Nugget

Be the Star You Are

Pretending is for little chicks,
not grown-up hens like us.
No need to hide inside a coop—
no need to squawk and fuss.
So stand up tall and crow a bit—
Quit wishing on a star.
Enjoy the way God made you:
"Special!" 'cause you are.

CHAPTER 33

Cackling and Laying Eggs

by Gracie Malone

One sultry afternoon in College Station during her senior year at Texas A&M, my friend Carolyn faced a dilemma. It was hot outside—hot enough to cook a two-egg omelet on the sidewalk without a skillet. Carolyn was also flat broke. If she turned on the air conditioner in her student apartment, she wouldn't have enough money at the end of the month to pay the electric bill. But she did have a shiny new credit card. Carolyn eyed that card, then did something she regrets to this day.

Dripping sweat, her hair hanging in strings, sundress sticking to the back of her legs, she jumped in the car and headed to town to purchase a fan. She parked in front, bolted through the double doors, waving plastic, and approached a nice looking college student clerk.

"Sir," she began, "does this store carry ovulating fans?"

The young gentleman didn't crack a grin as he pointed to a nearby shelf, then gently said, "Ma'am, I think they are called oscillating fans."

Carolyn wiped the sweat from her red-faced brow, purchased the fan, then ran lickety-split back to her car, all the while agonizing over one slip of the tongue and the difference a few little letters of the alphabet can make.

It's one thing when we mispronounce a word and embarrass ourselves. It's quite another when our words are misspelled and recorded in written form for all the world to see. Recently, my friend, Becky, wrote a story about me and mentioned my role as mentor to several younger women in our church. But instead of writing that I had nurtured them, she flatly stated, "Gracie has neutered many people."

I'm glad she let me proof that story before I lost all my friends. (By the way, Becky's husband, Scott, could have used a good editor when he wrote in an office memo that he had a very erotic schedule.) And our local newspaper could use help, too. They recently ran an article about Greenville's own public electric company. The headline read: "Pubic Power: A Tradition that Works in Greenville."

It seems women are especially prone to verbal goof-ups when we gather to "do lunch." Such was the case one day when Becky and I ate with our friend, Brenda, a Christian counselor. As we lingered over garlic spaghetti, the conversation turned toward the topic of Beanie Babies™. Becky confessed her brief interest in collecting them. Brenda, in true counselor form, interjected a few thoughts about how precious and meaningful the little critters are. Then I jumped in, "Why, I have two Beanies myself and both of them are indeed meaningful. Rebecca gave me the chicken named 'Strut,' and Becky gave me 'Gracie' for my birthday."

I sat back in my chair, feeling smug about my contribution to the small talk, until Brenda innocently asked, "Now, is 'Gracie' the bull?"

Becky folded in a fit of laughter. While Brenda wiped egg off her face, Becky continued, "'Gracie' is not a bull! Why, she's a graceful white swan Beanie." (By the way, the next day I received a book in the mail from Brenda. It was addressed to "Gracie the Swan.")

On another occasion, the waitress in a local restaurant laid an egg and didn't even know it. Since Becky and I are regulars at this cafeteria, the lady who serves coffee and tea knows us well—so well, in fact, that she felt comfortable giving Becky a sales pitch for a line of cosmetics. She slid her business card under the edge of Becky's plate and said, "Becky, you should try these products guaranteed to fill out wrinkles and keep you looking youthful. These wonderful creams make my skin soft and supple. I may look young, but I actually have grand-children." Then she patted her fluffy cheeks, nodded her head my direction, and zinged in the clincher, "Why, you'd never guess it, but I'm almost as old as her!"

Becky slipped the card in her purse and promised to call right away. Later, Becky admitted she wanted to buy a gallon of that stuff, but could only afford one two-ounce jar, which, I figure, is probably enough for a cute young chick like Becky.

Perhaps nobody has promoted the idea of looking good and using those good looks to please our husbands more than Marabel Morgan of *Total Woman* fame. Years ago, my friend, Wanda, read her book and started looking for opportunities to implement some of its suggestions. One morning when Wanda was feeling particularly amorous, the telephone rang. Allyson, four, outran her younger brother, Barry, to answer it. "Mom, it's Daddy," she said as she handed over the receiver.

Wanda, thinking her beloved husband, Lanny, was connected to the other end of the line, started spouting words in a sultry tone that would have made Marabel blush, "Hey, Sweetheart, do you have any plans for this evening? Talk to me, Baby."

Finally a timid voice answered, "Ma'am, this is the piano salesman. Do you want me to bring that piano over today?"

Wanda cleared her throat and managed a respectable sentence or two. When the guy showed up a few hours later, she met him outside and told him to forget that piano. I guess he'll never forget the phone call.

When Wanda told me that story, I couldn't help but think about the verse from Proverbs that promises, "When there are many words, transgression is unavoidable" (10:19 NASB). Wanda should have thought about that verse on another occasion a few years later.

At the school where she and her friend, Linda, teach, they observe several special events to promote school spirit, like "Back in Time Day" and "Bad Hair Day." One such day, they happened to drop in on the classroom of a new substitute teacher. Both Wanda and Linda were pleased to see that she'd wholeheartedly embraced the school's tradition. She was dressed in green, double knit, bell-bottom pants, and a double knit, plaid jacket with wide lapels, long pointed collar, and big plastic buttons. She wore black platform shoes. Perched on her head was a red, bouffant wig that looked like a hen's nest. Wanda and Linda went on and on about her outfit, "Look at you! Why, if you don't look like something from the '60s. Where did you get those clothes? I do declare!"

But, as they headed back out the door, Linda glanced over her shoulder and noticed a peculiar look on the teacher's face. Then in a moment of sudden realization, she tugged on Wanda's sleeve and gasped, "Oh, no! I think this is only 'Bad Hair Day.'"

In light of all the problems we gals have with our tongues, we'd do well to follow the example of another hen named Linda, my good friend Linda Gilbert. To keep from talking too much, she memorized a verse from Psalms, then added one little word of her own just to make the point clear. *Set a watch, O LORD, before my mouth; keep the door of my lips . . .* SHUT! (141:3 KJV).

> *Don't talk so much. You keep*
> *putting your foot in your mouth.*
> *Be sensible and turn off the flow!*
> Proverbs 10:19 TLB

Sizzling Hot Texas Omelet

Chicken Nugget

½ cup picante sauce
1 cup shredded Monterey Jack cheese
1 cup shredded cheddar cheese
6 eggs
1 8oz. carton sour cream
tomato wedges, fresh cilantro (optional)

Pour the ½ cup picante sauce into the bottom of a 10-inch quiche dish. Sprinkle cheeses over sauce. Blend eggs until smooth. Add sour cream. Pour the egg mixture over cheese. Bake uncovered in a 350-degree oven for 30 minutes or until a knife inserted near the center comes out clean. Drizzle with additional picante sauce. Top with tomato wedges and cilantro.

(May also be cooked on a hot Texas sidewalk. Time varies with the temperature.)

SECTION V

Spreading Your Wings

Courage for Growing Closer to God

CHAPTER 34

Pecking Out Dreams

by Becky Freeman

Our four children were tucked in bed and my husband was sleeping soundly as I tiptoed into my closet, sat down at my make-shift desk, and began pecking away at my dream. Somehow, someday, I would turn out a real book.

My mother and father had encouraged my efforts by giving me a marvelous invention for my birthday—a word processor. All day I waited patiently for the sun to go down and the house to grow quiet so I could slip, uninterrupted, into the fascinating world of words. I thought nothing of sitting for hours, completely engrossed, as I let my fingers do the talking.

"There are three kinds of people in this world," I typed one night. "You have your right-brain creative types, your left-brain organizers, and then, you have those peculiar people who cannot seem to locate cerebral matter in either hemisphere. I am whichever brain it is that can organize her thoughts on paper, be a member of numerous honor societies, and still manage to wear her dress inside out all day without noticing."

As I pondered my own scattered brain, I couldn't help but think of my very "together" little sister, Rachel. So I wrote, "When we were children living at home, Rachel's belongings were so organized that I could not filch so much as one piece of chocolate candy from her mammoth Easter basket without being called to account for it.

"Even our taste in clothes reflected our different personalities. As we grew to be teenagers, Rachel opted for a few well-tailored, quality suits. I, on the other hand, had a closet full of bargains with lots of ruffles, lace, and color."

As we grew into adults, the differences between us was even more obvious. So I wrote about how Rachel and her meticulous husband bought a chic condominium filled with beautiful furniture, in white. And how my husband and I bought a tiny cabin in the woods and filled it to the brim with four children and garage sale furniture. Each piece was selected for its intrinsic ability to disguise peanut butter and jelly.

Then I captured, with computer ink, the contrasting stories of our initiations into motherhood. I had dramatic, wacky, agonizing home births that seemed to go on for days—even weeks. My sister, conversely, started her labor at a convenient 3:00 in the afternoon and gave birth around 6:00 P.M.—just in time to celebrate the "birthday" with a commemorative steak dinner, served precisely at 7:00 P.M., as my newborn nephew, Trevor, snoozed soundly all night in his designer nightie.

Who would have dreamed that the story I wrote about me and my sister, in those wee hours of the morning, would ever "come out of the closet" and end up in a real book? Of all the things I'll ever write, *Worms in My Tea* may always be the most special to me, for it was my "firstborn" book. When it debuted in bookstores, the first person to call and cheer and celebrate the occasion was—you guessed it—my life-sized opposite, my sister Rachel. For as different as we may be, we are kindred spirits in ways that matter most—like being each other's number one best fan and solace.

When Scott and I went through a rough time in our marriage it was, most often, my sister I wanted to confide in. Then came the evening when Rachel hit her own emotional wall and phoned me from her home in Virginia. When I picked up the phone, heard her voice, and asked how she was, Rachel tearfully replied, "Really messed up," and I said, "Welcome to the human race" and then we laughed and we cried and we talked for four hours—as only two sisters-in-crisis can.

One November, we took a "sisters only" trip to Tennessee, where I would discover that Rachel and I had more in common than I had originally supposed. Rachel and I headquartered, during our vacation, at a gorgeous bed and breakfast with the enticing name "The Rose Garden." We'd play all day, then come home to our cozy bungalow and a roaring fire in the evenings. Sometimes we'd dash out to the hot tub under the starlit sky and as we soaked, we also shared from our hearts.

"Rachel," I asked one chilly evening as I eased luxuriously into the vat of steaming water, "what are your dreams? What would you love to do someday—perhaps when Trevor gets a little older?"

"I almost hate to tell you," Rachel replied dreamily, from her corner of the hot tub.

"Why?"

"Because I'm afraid you'll think I'm copying you. And because I don't know if I can do it as well as you and Mother."

"Rachel," I said, my eyes wide with excitement, "you want to write, don't you?"

"I've thought about it."

"You can do it. You absolutely can do it. Look, it just runs in the family. Aunt Etta was the first writer. Then Mother. Then me. And now you must be destined to be the next family writer!"

"I'm nervous."

"Who isn't?"

"You'll help me?"

"I'd love to!"

"You'll be honest?"

"I promise."

"But gentle?"

"Of course."

About two months after our trip to Nashville, my fax machine spit out a long line of paper. I picked it up, and to my delight, saw that it was Rachel's first attempt at an article. It touched me that she'd chosen to write about our *sister trip,* but I have to admit, I silently prayed, "Lord, please let this be good." If the writing was bad, I had no backup response.

I needn't have worried. Writing must be inscribed in our family's genetic makeup. Not only could my sister write, she could write well and she could write funny! I chuckled as I read Rachel's description of me floating around the hot tub "like a happy marshmallow." I laughed aloud at the part where she wrote about herself, imagining the next morning's newspaper headline reading: "Two Sisters Found Floating in Hot Tub— Brought Down by a Deadly Strain of Bacteria."

Now that we're grown up, nothing has really changed! Rachel still worries about deadly bacteria, while I'm thinking, *Let's dive in.* She leans toward the tailored look, while I brake for fru-fru. And she still prefers pain-free, on-schedule childbirth, while I, for some reason, insist on natural, cozy, excruciatingly painful home births. She's "Ethan Allen™" and "pocket organizers." I'm "early garage sale" and "running late." Rachel uses left-brain logic, and I'm right-brained ridiculous.

We're as opposite as two sisters can be—except that we love each other fiercely. And now, we have something else in common. In the wee hours of the morning, you can find both of us tap-typing away—caught up in the "world of words." Of course, Rachel is probably sitting on an "Early American" office chair (white), while I compose my articles seated cross-legged on a jelly-stained stool.

In truth, it matters not where any of us perch to do our pecking. What matters is that when we are ready to fly into a new venture, we have at least one sister of the soul—whether related by blood or simply by love—who comes alongside to encourage. We all need a cheerleader standing by with pom-poms and enthusiasm to spare as we take off on the fragile wings of our dreams.

> *"If you can?" said Jesus. "Everything*
> *is possible for him who believes."*
> Mark 9:23

Chicken Nugget

One day I opened the mailbox to discover Rachel had sent me an inspiring little book called *All Things Are Possible*. "What can one little, ordinary person accomplish?" we sometimes wonder. May these quotes be your cheerleader today as you gather the courage to begin a new dream.

"If you can't feed a hundred people, then feed just one."
Mother Teresa

" . . . if one advances confidently in the direction of his dreams, and endeavors to live the life which he has imagined, he will meet with a success unexpected in common hours."
Henry David Thoreau

"Pessimism is a waste of time."
Norman Cousins

"There are many wonderful things that will never be done if you do not do them."
Honorable Charles D. Gill

"Hold fast to dreams, for if dreams die, life is a broken-winged bird that cannot fly."
Langston Hughes

CHAPTER 35

To Crow or Not to Crow

by Rebecca Barlow Jordan

When I was younger, I attended writers' conferences primarily to prove that I wasn't chicken about writing. I still remember one editor's words of wisdom: "Don't send your manuscripts in a pizza box. Don't leave chocolate smudges on the paper. Who told you that you could write?" After one conference, another question kept floating around in my mind like a lone feather.

Prior to that particular weekend, I had felt the constant pain of rejection even in the midst of a good year of sales. This time, I had preened my manuscript for weeks and really felt like I had something to crow about. When the day finally arrived, I wagged my proposal around to each class at the conference. Writing furiously, I devoured tasty feed from each speaker. I cornered editors, pushed my literary wares, and trailed after instructors, hoping to glean a few nuggets of truth that fell from their hallowed beaks.

At lunch break when I entered the cafeteria, I fell in line with every other "wannabe" writer, like chicks following after their mother hens. I targeted one particular instructor and huddled close, waiting for an appropriate moment to banter back and forth about the features of my project. In short, I was consumed with my own agenda.

Yet inside me a contradiction was emerging. In one ear, I heard my father's humorous admonitions: "He that tooteth not his own horn, the same shall not be tooted!" In the other ear, my childhood teacher's voice whispered, "Humble yourself, humble yourself." Like an inexperienced acrobat dangling by one leg in the middle of the tightrope—I struggled for balance.

Embarrassed by my own lack of sensitivity, I observed a fellow journalist as she reached out to a lonely young writer: "Come with me. This workshop will be perfect for you." Professionals spoke with unaffected joy about the motivation in their writing. I listened in awe. I observed patient coordinators surrender personal conference time, offering helpful words to wandering conferees and hesitant chicks. Each in their own way, by their very actions and words, said, "There you are," not "Here I am."

However, one gregarious hen, with her wings flapping wildly, followed an editor into the ladies' restroom. I watched silently as she parked in front of the speaker's closed door. I could hardly believe what she did next. Still clucking away, the writer stooped down and shoved her manuscript under the editor's bathroom stall. "Here's my story," she crowed. "It's great. God gave it to me—and I *know* you'll love it."

I kept clicking on a mental picture of that rude scene, recalling the wise words from another communicator, a Master Teacher—the Real Pro. And I wondered, "What would He say and do?" I remembered reading how He spoke with authority when others—even His own parents—questioned His actions and motives. He offered no putdowns, but with genuine confidence, this young Man-Child clearly interpreted His bold actions without hesitation. In my mind, from town to town, I shadowed this Teacher, observing His kind and loving gestures to the lonely, the downtrodden, the insecure, the brash. He never ridiculed others; nor did He promote Himself for selfish gains. He was balanced.

Shy? Not Jesus. Yet He was gentle enough to comfort a frightened child with heaven's wings. Assertive? Yes, but always with the command of a controlled spirit, tempered by His Father's love. Was He boastful? Never of Himself, only of His Father. Yet wannabe followers flocked to this remarkable Teacher—He Who carved out time for the sick and fearlessly challenged the beautiful and arrogant, He Who listened to the friendless and fed the hungry.

The dilemma may always challenge me as a writer—to crow or not to crow? Is it nobler to speak up boldly, even when we may feel inside, like humble amateurs? After all, if *we* don't believe in our hen scratchings, who will? Or should we take up arms against a sea of pride, cowering under false humility as we listen to the voice of our worst critic—self? To do that, or to compare ourselves with more successful authors, might trigger discouragement: *Who needs my words, anyway?* If I squawk too much, I'm branded "cocky." If I tuck my tail feathers, I'm called "chicken." That struggle is not unique to writers but extends to the boardroom, the classroom, our workplace, home, or church.

I remembered the great King David. For years in quietness and confidence, he composed his songs to the Good Shepherd. And then one day, someone heard David's sweet music. Surely in his severe depression, King Saul could benefit from this musician. So someone told the king, and the king called for David. The result? A best-seller! And millions of people today still flock to his soothing Psalms. And all this happened to David without self-promotion.

And then I heard an inner, inaudible voice. Perhaps it originated from my own field of dreams whispering to me through the massive office doors of editors (not bathroom stalls). Or maybe it was a divine nugget from God Himself, intended only for my ears: "Write it, and they will buy! Listen, and I will teach you."

Years later, someone asked me to teach at a writers' conference. When eager beaks flew open, I tried to drop in helpful nuggets of inspiration and encouragement. When young chicks followed me around, I gave them this advice: "Finding that balance between 'crowing' and 'clucking' will always be difficult—especially after you've tasted a few morsels of success. Because of our humanness, most of us will always struggle with mixed motives. But with practice and experience, you can learn to hone your God-given talent and feel good about telling those editors, 'I'm eggcited about this project. I believe it has potential!'"

But the best thing I can tell novice writers is what I learned the hard way: "Like a musician returning for basic theory lessons, I go back to the basics often—back to a classroom taught by a humble Shepherd—a lowly Carpenter. There I can find the answers—and the confidence I really need.

"Let him who boasts boast in the Lord."
For it is not the one who commends himself who
is approved, but the one whom the Lord commends.
2 Corinthians 10:17,18

Chicken Nugget

Heavenly Eggs-pectations

If only for man's praise

we write,

or monetary fee,

we may be disappointed

when we reach

eternity.

CHAPTER 36

One Chick Serving God with All Her Hat/Heart

by Fran Caffey Sandin

"Jim!" I yelled, while bobbing up and down in Lake Tawakoni. "I just remembered"—glub, glub—"I have to play the organ for Tammy's wedding later this afternoon!"

"Don't worry," my rooster responded confidently. "I'll get you there in time."

Jim and I were having a good time practicing our sailing skills that brisk, sunshiny March day until Mother Nature took a big breath and puffed hard against our sails. Unable to recover from the dramatic heel, the centerboarder capsized. *Splash!* We fell into the lake. With strands of wet hair dangling over my eyes, I thanked the Lord for life preservers.

Jim and I tried to right the small craft, but a heavy gust caught the sails and flipped the boat upside down once again, this time breaking the mast. Later, we learned that wind warning flags had been posted on the lake, but we hadn't noticed, hadn't even wondered why we were the only boat out.

Just as we were pondering what to do next, a welcome "putt-putt" sound came near. Two men saw our distress and motored out to help us. I've never really thought of fishermen as smelly angels, but that day, as far as I was concerned, they wore halos.

Our two rescuers pulled us into their boat, hauled our broken-masted rig to shore, and then scooted across the water to our lake house pier where I jumped out, shook my feathers, and ran shivering into the cabin. Jim and I quickly drank a cup of hot soup (more for warmth than for hunger) and then I showered, blew my hair dry, and changed into a dress.

Jim raced us to the church, as if we were on the last lap of the Indy-500. As we careened into the parking lot, I double-checked my makeup; then hopped out of the car, ran down the aisle, slid onto the organ bench, and began playing the sedate prelude at the appointed time. A large crowd gathered, but no one ever suspected the organist almost missed the wedding.

Musical hens always have stories to tell. As a young girl, I studied at the "Hoard Switch Conservatory" in East Texas, namely Smith Chapel. There our country church pianist, affectionately known as Miss Willie, enthusiastically and faithfully played the old upright.

While performing (oops, I mean playing) she wore a large, floppy, wide-brimmed hat, complete with flowers all around. I was amazed at how she could play, sing loudly, and keep her head moving—all at the same time; and I watched with wide eyes every Sunday as her headpiece rhythmically bounced up and down. When she took off on the chorus of "I'll Fly Away" I just knew those posies would turn loose and take flight in all directions—but they never did.

Although I could never duplicate Miss Willie's unique style, I knew she played with all her hat. She never did anything half-heartedly. As a church organist, I have often remembered her example (even though I don't wear a hat).

Now as a woman of the '90s, juggling many responsibilities has become quite a challenge. In addition to playing the organ and writing, I also work part-time as a nurse in my husband's urology office. One day before leaving the office to play for a funeral, I absentmindedly grabbed a three-ring binder, popped it open, inserted my plastic-sleeved music, and headed out to the church.

Can you imagine how horrified I was after the service to discover the front cover sported a large, colorful anatomical illustration of the kidneys, the ureter, the bladder, and the urethra! I had extended the notebook wide open directly onto a clear, acrylic music stand for all to see. I'd like to believe that my presentation was so powerful that no one noticed—or maybe they thought the drawing was a rather weird flower arrangement. But I'm certainly more careful these days.

Through the years, I've learned to play the organ under many adverse circumstances. Like the wedding when I was finishing the last piece of the prelude before the processional and a man tiptoed behind me and whispered in my ear—"Just keep on playing. The family forgot the video camera and they've gone home to get it." "Sure," I responded, wondering how many different ways I could play "Oh Perfect Love" before I began to sound like a broken record.

Then there was the little church in another state where the organ had not been serviced in years. The pipes were for decoration only and about every third note played. Another problem surfaced quickly. The thick, shag carpet met the linoleum halfway under the bench where I was sitting—so as I played the pedals with my feet, the bench rocked back and forth over the hump. Concentrating on the music was nothing compared to riding that bucking bench! After the first fifteen minutes, I was ready to be crowned as the local rodeo queen.

Although I've had my share of unusual experiences, they can't compare to the dramatic stories I've heard at instructional workshops—like the bride who brushed too close to the candles and her hair caught fire. Fortunately, she was not hurt.

Or this one. After the guests had been seated for the wedding at 7:00 P.M., the pastor announced the time for the ceremony had been changed to 10:00 P.M. so the bride's mother could finish sewing the bridal dress! The organist even left the church and went to their home to help with the project. Surprisingly, most of the guests and even the groom returned at 10:00 P.M. for the wedding. Never a dull moment for musicians.

I wish I could play music perfectly, but it rarely happens. However, through practice, practice, and more practice, I have learned to play with confidence, wrong notes and all. Even sour notes can be played boldly, and if I move on with confidence and finesse, it may seem the arrangement just took an unusual turn.

Long ago I realized that God has given me an uncommon love for music, and it is vital for my soul to express it. Although it does take stamina and requires a great deal of practice, using my talent energizes me. When I'm playing, I don't really think about all the people who are listening. I think about God as my only audience—sitting in the sanctuary. Then, like Miss Willie, I play for Him with all my heart (but still, no hat).

Whatever you do, work at it with all your heart,
as working for the Lord, not for men, since you
know that you will receive an inheritance from the
Lord as a reward. It is the Lord Christ you are serving.
Colossians 3:23,24

Chicken Nugget

What is Your Gift?

What is your gift, dear hen?

Is it being a mother or being a friend?

Is it baking a cake or visiting the sick?

Speaking for crowds or performing a trick?

Is it playing a harp or drums of percussion?

Sweeping the floor or leading discussions?

Whatever your gift, be it great or small,

You honor Him when you give it your all.

CHAPTER 37

Fowl Thinkin'

by Gracie Malone

Near the Grapevine depot our son, Matt, turned onto a muddy road, eager to demonstrate the traction capabilities of his new four-wheel drive vehicle to his young brood. Eight-year-old Luke egged his dad on; Mary Catherine, three, giggled and cheered; and Abigail, three months, cooed contentedly from her car seat. But six-year-old Connor held both armrests in a death grip. With his unique personality and a disposition Matt describes as "a bit on the dark side," Connor views life more seriously.

When Matt turned to console his panicky son, the truck slid sideways, slipped into deep mire, and stuck. He switched gears and stepped on the gas pedal. The engine roared. Connor burst into tears. The other kids gasped.

"It's okay, guys. Connor, don't cry." Matt's confident tone seemed to have the desired calming effect on the vehicle's occupants. Then turning to Connor, Matt posed the question he often asks himself when things are not going well, "What's the worst thing that could happen?"

Connor thought for a few moments, then droned out his answer. "We . . . could . . . starve . . . to . . . death . . . and . . . die!"

Matt patted Connor on the back. "No, man, the worst thing that could happen here is, we get out of the car, get our feet muddy, and walk home."

Connor wiped his tears on his sleeve, then slid his arms around his daddy's neck. Matt opened the door. Just as he started to "take the muddy plunge," a farmer who had seen their predicament shoved his tractor into high gear and raced to the rescue. Their hero in overalls hooked a chain on the vehicle's bumper and pulled them toward higher ground.

When Matt shared this story over the phone, I thought, *Sometimes I feel just like Connor.* In the mudslides of life, when my feet start to slip, I look at the circumstances and think the worst.

One morning, three weeks after back surgery, I looked at my six-inch-long incision in the mirror and then sat down on the bed, totally disheartened. The scar was swollen and tender. Since I was already taking antibiotics, I wondered, *Why does my back still hurt so badly?*

The next morning, I opened my Bible to the Old Testament book of Habakkuk. In this obscure little book, a prophet with a funny name, has recorded one of the deepest truths in all of Scripture: "The just shall live by his faith" (Habakkuk 2:4 KJV). As I thought about those words written centuries ago they became a personal message from God to me. I needed to live by faith. Sending an SOS heavenward, I cried, "Lord, please tell me what to do."

I didn't hear an audible voice, but immediately, I knew exactly what to do. I called the doctor's office. "I want the doctor to check my back. May I come now?" I was surprised when the nurse answered, "Yes." When I arrived, the doctor examined me and suggested I check into the hospital. After I settled into a room, techs escorted me downstairs for an MRI.

The test revealed pockets of infection spreading close to the bone. My doctor would have to perform surgery again. When he said they would "wash out the wound," I couldn't help but cringe. I thought about our waterpick, then the "power wash" we use to clean the driveway. To say I felt chicken hearted would have been an understatement. I was downright scared!

I called John, a family friend, the one we always call when things get crazy. He reminded me that "the Lord is my Shepherd" and prayed that "goodness and mercy" would follow me like "two sheep dogs." As I drifted off to sleep, visions of two shaggy dogs romping through green pastures brought a sense of peace.

Early the next morning friends called to encourage me. They each ended their conversation with, "Gracie, may I pray for you?" God was saying clearly, "I am with you. I am with you. I am with you." My faith sprouted wings! As they wheeled me into the operating room, I felt wrapped in God's comfort blanket of love.

The surgery went well. Although the lab tests confirmed a serious infection that would require six weeks of IV treatment, we had caught it in the early stages. The doctor knew exactly which antibiotic to prescribe. God had answered our prayers. My steps of faith had been rewarded.

Throughout my hospital stay, friends and family members became messengers of God's love. On Sunday, my family came to visit—one husband, three sons, one daughter-in-law, and five little grandchicks. After all the hugs and kisses, my room became a zoo.

Luke and Connor, fascinated by my automatic bed, sent me up and down like a yo-yo on a string. But, try as they would, that bed would not lift me all the way to the ceiling! Montana started spouting lines from *Bedtime Bubba,* the birthday present we had given him. I played peek-a-boo with sixteen-month-old Abigail.

When her sweet face popped up over the foot of my bed, I could, with one silly grin, send her running back into her daddy's arms.

Then Joe, our Papa Joe, the one sane person who could have stopped the madness, started blowing air into surgical gloves, making balloons that looked like fat hands with stiff fingers. The kids went wild.

While all this was going on, four-year-old Mary Catherine busied herself playing nurse. She donned a pair of surgical gloves; then, with rubber fingertips flapping crazily, she proceeded to examine me. First, she gently pulled my bottom eyelid down. "Doctor," I asked, "are my eyes okay?" In quite the professional manner, Mary Catherine nodded and pronounced them, "Sparkley!" Next, she studiously looked up my nose. When I inquired of its condition, she placed one hand on her hip, and proclaimed, "It's nosey!"

Mary Catherine had one more thing to say—something just between us girls, something so strictly confidential that she leaned close to my ear, cupped her little hand, and whispered, "Grandma Gracie, *where* is your makeup?"

After an hour, I sent another spiritual SOS. "Lord, move mightily in the hearts of my kids. May they gather their chicks and head for the roost!" My prayer was answered right away.

A few days later I was home. During the long period of treatment and recovery, I remembered God's faithfulness and often pondered Habakkuk's words: *The just shall live by his faith.* And whenever I felt stuck in a bog, I thought about Connor. Then I'd slip my arms around my Heavenly Father's neck and hold on tight.

He will make my feet like hinds' feet, and he
will make me to walk upon mine high places.
Habakkuk 3:19 KJV

Chicken Nugget

FAITH Is . . .

1. The steppingstones in the bogs of life.
2. The solid ground beneath every muddy road.
3. Knowing that God always has a tractor and a chain.

CHAPTER 38

Approaching the Roost

by Rebecca Barlow Jordan

"Daddy, do you think God would give me a new swimming pool if I asked Him for one?" questioned our oldest daughter, Valerie. She was anxious to get back in the water. Summer had arrived, bringing with it a blazing Arizona heat wave. We had a steel wall left over from our last wading pool, but no liner. Pools never lasted long at our house.

Two years before, I'd been splashing around in three feet of water, when I accidentally stumbled backward, hitting the side of the pool. A rush of water knocked me and the retaining wall down, ripping the liner in the process. We replaced the liner the following year.

Unfortunately, that pool also met an untimely death. In a moment of temporary insanity, we gave our daughters a second dog—a furry, black puppy for Christmas—breed unknown. The girls affectionately named the new puppy "Nibbles"—and oh how he lived up to his name. Clothing hung out in the sunshine was shredded and fringed by canine teeth; carefully grown, mature grapevines shriveled after being chewed off at the ground. Even the corners of the house bore strange designs, artistically gnawed by our beloved doggie. We should have dubbed our pet, "Beaver." Nothing was safe from this compulsive chewer.

The real gizzard buster came the summer after Nibbles munched his way into our lives. We returned home one scorching day to find our beloved oasis in shambles. Nibbles had crunched completely through the extension cord to the pool's filtration system and made confetti of the pool's liner. In that last fatal crunch, our swimming pool bit the dust.

Now, two years later, Valerie was asking her daddy to pray for a new pool while I'm sure visions of Nibbles' disasters danced in his head. At this stage of our lives, we were limiting our purchases to the three big necessities—food, shelter, and toilet paper. A complete new pool system would blow our budget, and we had no nest egg filling up with extra funds. Upon realizing this, our daughter had simply turned her request over to a higher authority.

Her father answered Valerie's question, "Will God give me a new swimming pool?" with his usual wisdom. "Well, if you plan to share the pool with your friends and not use it selfishly, I'm sure God will honor your prayer. He says He'll give us the desires of our hearts if we put Him first."

Satisfied with her dad's response, Valerie strutted off, certain of an impending miracle. However, weeks passed and not even a mirage of a pool appeared in our backyard. I thought about telling my daughter, "Honey, maybe we're counting our chickens before they hatch." Instead, I casually mentioned that she might want to start her own savings account to buy the pool. "Maybe that's the way God wants to answer your prayer." I added. "If you keep saving, perhaps by next summer you'll have enough money—at least enough for a small pool."

Valerie's frown told me this was not the sort of miracle she had in mind, and I wasn't convinced either. So we would sweat it out—and wait. A few weeks later, a good friend called me. "Rebecca, we just bought the kids a new pool," she said. "They wanted something bigger. By the way, we don't need our old one—and it still works. The pump, liner, and all the parts are intact. Would your girls like a pool this summer?"

Silence.

"Are you okay?" asked my friend.

I grinned and shot up a quick prayer of thanksgiving for my angelic hen friend. Later, I relayed the good news to Valerie. "God really did answer your prayer, didn't He?"

"And the pool is free?" she questioned in disbelief. "Wow, Mom! God can do anything, can't He?"

When our friends delivered the pool the following week, we assembled it and filled it with water in a few short hours. From the kitchen window, I watched the girls dive and splash like a couple of little ducks, showering each other with refreshing streams. That summer, God boosted my confidence tenfold in His willingness to provide not only our needs—but also the desires of our childlike hearts—just like He promised in Ezekiel 34:26, *I will send down showers in season; there will be showers of blessing.*

P.S. A few weeks later, I thought about my daughter's bold confession. God can do anything, can't He! I decided to test this truth with a secret prayer of my own. I asked God to find a new home for our dog Nibbles—anywhere but ours. Sure enough, God CAN do anything. The last we heard, Nibbles was gnawing his way into the new owner's heart and home.

Let us then approach the throne of grace
with confidence, so that we may receive mercy
and find grace to help us in our time of need.
Hebrews 4:16

How to Approach God's Roost, Especially if You Are a Chicken

1. Find a quiet coop to meet alone with God consistently (Psalm 5:3).

2. Begin confidently with a time of crowing—boasting in the Lord (Psalm 34:2).

3. Share a time of remembrance—thanking God for the delicious seed He provides, for tucking you under His wings, for making you one of His brood, and for the good things He is hatching out in your life (Psalm 106:1).

4. Let down your ruffled feathers—give God any worries, concerns, or special petitions of your own, as well as the needs of your chicken friends (Philippians 4:6).

5. Keep a hen pen and notebook ready for pecking out prayer request lists. Record the date you pray and how and when God answers (Exodus 17:14).

6. Ask the Lord to pluck out anything fowl—whatever is displeasing to Him. Forgiven chickens make contented hens (Psalm 139:23,24).

7. Pray with a little chick's faith, in the name of Jesus— things that are according to His will. Assure Him that your chief desire is to let Him rule the roost (Luke 22:42).

CHAPTER 39

My Grade "A" Label

by Gracie Malone

When my mother gave birth to me in an old bungalow near Prosper, Texas, it was pouring down rain. Several buckets strategically placed on the bedroom floor caught drips from the old, leaky roof.

Daddy was able to plow through the deep mud in a borrowed Model A Ford to get my Aunt Grace, Mom's younger sister, who lived in the nearby town of Altoga. Grace, a seventeen-year-old newlywed, was willing to help, even though, like Prissy of *Gone with the Wind* fame, she knew absolutely nothing about "birthin' babies."

The story goes that my dad left Grace there with my mother in the throes of labor while he chugged into McKinney to fetch Dr. Robason, the county's "baby specialist." Shortly after the doctor arrived, I made my Grace-ful entry into the world. With one final heave-ho, my mother deposited me into the doctor's hands, who in turn placed me in the trembling arms of my Aunt Grace.

Inexperienced though she was, Grace bathed me, pinned a fresh cloth diaper on my bottom, and placed me in the arms of my exhausted but happy mother. Mom took one look at me, another at her little sister, and named me Gracie—Gracie Allen.

She had no idea that in the glitzy world of vaudeville, a pair of comedians named George Burns and Gracie Allen, were becoming one of America's most famous duos. And there was no way she could have known how our identical names would cause me trouble in years to come.

The other Gracie Allen was a ditzy housewife, described by her husband, George, as "lovable but confused." She said crazy things like, "The grapefruit we grew this year were so big, it only takes eight of them to make a dozen." On another occasion, she confessed cheating on her driver's license test by copying the car in front of her.

Nevertheless, I grew up feeling privileged just knowing I was named after my beautiful and fun-loving Aunt Grace. Still there were times when I did not like my name. I hated it when the pigtailed daughter of my Grandpa's farmhand called me "Grassy." I didn't like my name when my brothers called me "Grapes." And, I really hated being "Gracie Allen" during my teen years. Every time I introduced myself, I got a crazy reaction.

As a sophomore in high school, my first serious boyfriend was planning to be a preacher. So I decided I needed to learn to play the piano. I fantasized that we'd get married, he'd preach, I'd play, we'd sing, and the whole world would repent and turn to God. I cherished this dream, even though my musical training was limited to a somewhat-less-than-accomplished tooting of the French horn in the eighth-grade band, and singing the alto line from the *Baptist Hymnal* in my church's youth choir. Still, I dreamed of playing the piano.

One day I mustered up enough courage to ask my daddy if he would buy me the piano that would change my life forever. I was thrilled when he answered, "Check some prices." The next day after school, I thumbed through the yellow pages, made a few phone calls, and found a real deal. But as I talked to the salesman, he grew impatient with my bargaining tactics and my lack of savvy about musical things. I promised to bring my daddy to the store and wrote down the address.

I should have known what was coming at the end of our bewildering conversation when the clerk asked for my name. I gulped hard and said, "This is Gracie Allen."

"Well!" he shouted, "When you come in, just ask for George Burns!" Then he slammed down the receiver.

When Daddy came home, I told him what had happened, then burst into tears. He called the salesman. "Sir," I overheard him say curtly, "my daughter's name *really is* Gracie Allen. She's crying because you hung up on her."

Later my dad reported that the flabbergasted salesman apologized. He thought he was being pranked. "If you'll come by the store, I'll give you a really good deal on that piano."

"We'll be right there," Daddy said, then with tongue in cheek, he added, "by the way, my name is George. George Allen, that is, and don't you hang up on me."

We bought that piano. I took lessons for nine months and learned to play a few hymns in the key of C before I decided the preacher boy was not the love of my life after all. I sold the piano and socked the money away in the bank.

A few years later I met Joe. When he asked me to marry him, my first thought—well, maybe my second thought—was, *Now I won't be Gracie Allen anymore.* I liked the sound of Gracie Malone. It had a nice literary ring, suitable for an aspiring writer. But I liked my name even more several years later when I understood its spiritual meaning. Grace—the compassion, kindness, and unmerited favor of God which He grants to His children.

Today, I know that every blessing I receive is a gift of God's grace. When I encounter difficulties or face some great challenge, God always provides grace so that I can handle it. In times of weakness or inadequacy, God gives me strength and power to do His will.

How could I ever forget that "God's grace is sufficient for me" (2 Corinthians 12:9)? My name is a constant reminder.

I have redeemed you; I have called
you by name; you are Mine!
Isaiah 43:1 NASB

Chicken Nugget

Folks with Funny Names

Wyn Shields

Jay Walker

Rusty Pipes

Snow White

Olive Green

Penny Money

CHAPTER 40

Grace for Sunday Chickens

by Becky Freeman

A year or so ago, my husband and I joined several other couples in forming a different sort of church—a place for people who don't like church, or are intimidated by formal services and stained glass doors. One of our men, an energetic Tigger kind of guy named Steve, located a gymnasium, complete with a full-sized swimming pool. Steve, being a rather jolly and persuasive soul, somehow convinced the lot of us that this would be a cool place to have church.

Within days, five families armed ourselves with paint, pliers, sheetrock, and hammers, as daddies on down to kids proceeded to turn a large, cold, metal building into a respectable sanctuary.

Amazingly, in less than three weeks, the black and red walls were painted a soft ivory and the cold cement floors were carpeted light green. We built a platform up front, as well as a wall to separate the worship center from the swimming hole. Though it still looked more like First Church of the Gymnasium than First Presbyterian or First Baptist, it was ours and we loved it.

As one might imagine, our services have also been somewhat unique. Steve leads the worship, which is a mixture of contemporary Christian music with guitars, drums, and keyboard as backup. Some traditional hymns and an occasional inspirational jazz number are also thrown in. Eclectic is us.

We recently had our first baptismal service—yes, in the swimming pool. It was hard not to grin as each child to be baptized literally swam out to the pastor for the liturgical ceremony.

Soon our teenagers caught the spirit of freedom and creativity and formed their own ministry to the community. My son, Zeke, along with the help of a handful of other teenagers started a "Soul Cafe" night, every other Saturday. Kids come to relax with a cup of cappuccino, play games, listen to Christian music, visit with other teens, and participate in a drama—or even swing dance! As many as a hundred kids have come on a Saturday for an evening of wholesome fun. It's enough to make any old parishioner wish he or she were young again.

If Steve is a young and enthusiastic Tigger kind of leader, then our pastor, Coyle, is a mixture of wise old Owl and friendly Pooh. (In fact, I suggested we call our fellowship "The Church on Pooh Corner," but "Grace Community" won the title.)

Pastor Coyle shares each Sunday from his heart, his life experience, and Scripture. He sits down to teach, the same way Jesus so often did when He taught on the grassy hills of Jerusalem. It's a position that invites us to join in worship together. It says, "I'm among you, not above you. I'm here to open my heart, not to hit you on the head with guilt."

Having spent years as a hospital chaplain and a counselor to other pastors, one of the truths Pastor Coyle has gleaned and shared with us time and again is, "People are just so hungry for a little affirmation." He understands the simple needs of the human heart, no matter their status in life. So relaxed is he at this retirement stage of life, that after his sermons he invites insights and comments from our small congregation. All comments are welcome, and each person is treated as a special, beloved child of God in this family living room of faith.

So our fledgling church is becoming, with each passing week, more and more like a true family, with all its wonders and oddities. From its inception, we prayed that as a church family, we would exemplify the "What Would Jesus Do?" mentality, opening our hearts to anyone and everyone. We imagined unwed mothers, burned-out Christians, and hurting saints would come to our services looking for loving acceptance. But never in our wildest dreams did we visualize Don.

Within a week after we moved into our church building, an old blue van pulled up in the parking lot and died. Out of the rickety vehicle stumbled a Robin Williams look-alike with wild, untamed hair and a matted beard. We soon realized that his thoughts were as hard to follow as a runaway train.

Many of our rag-tag group tried to reach out to Don, but his fragrance and his wandering mind kept most of us at bay. Conversations with Don were wild things. His replies to questions, though often eloquent, made no sense. His brain fired on the oddest of cylinders. In private, I think most of us would agree that it was more fun to read warmhearted stories about the church reaching out to the less fortunate, than to actually sit in the same pew with a homeless person—up close and personal.

Over months of hit and run conversations, we learned Don spent some time in the military and in a mental hospital. We surmised drugs may have been part of his past, perhaps having fried a few vital synapses. His days consisted of walking miles and miles to town and back. He loved living independently, out of his van.

Though we gave Don occasional gifts of food and clothes, he never asked for a handout other than the use of the church's water hydrant. Men prayed with him but could never really tell if Don understood that God loved him. In time, we determined that he was basically harmless and doing the best he could with what he had to work with. In fact, though sometimes lonely, Don seemed happy.

He attended church regularly in his favorite tattered jeans with a rope for a belt and an old T-shirt. As we stood to sing praise songs one morning, Scott elbowed me quietly and whispered, "Becky, look." Don's eyes were closed and his hands raised. After the service, Scott gave him his own Bible, fully aware that Don could not read. When I questioned this, Scott answered softly, "I just want Don to know somebody really cares about him." But Scott was tough on Don, too, always encouraging him to work hard for a better life.

Then one Sunday in December, seven months after our first "Don encounter," Scott offered to buy our homeless friend a bus ticket home to visit his mother, whom he'd not seen in three years.

"Want to go with me to take Don to the bus station?" Scott asked me later that afternoon. Reluctantly, I agreed.

As we drove in the night fog, we spied Don standing near the road with his bags packed, excited as a kid. Just before we pulled up to the curb Scott asked, "Becky, can we take him out to dinner?"

"Couldn't we just take him through the nearest fast-food drive-through window?" I asked, hopefully.

"Becky," Scott answered, shaking his head, "you can do this." And so we ate dinner out at a lovely restaurant. Me, Scott, and a hairy, homeless man. With every sip of hot coffee and bite of enchilada, Don seemed to glow with happiness.

As we drove from the restaurant to the bus station, Don spoke from the back seat, his voice wavering. "I know I'm not your son or anything but I kind of feel like it."

Moments later the three of us were walking toward a loud, idling Greyhound, and I wrapped my arms around Don's bushy neck in a spontaneous good-bye gesture. For a moment, he just stood there beaming; then he reached for Scott and hugged him, and back again to me for one last embrace. I wondered how long it had been since Don had felt a human touch.

And I also knew that Don was not the only one who was touched. In that sweet brief moment in time, Scott and I knew that God had touched us. We were doing what Jesus might have done—only Jesus would have done it with less hesitation, more abandonment of love.

In truth, loving the unlovely is exactly what God did for us. And this is, in fact, what being His living, loving, breathing Church is all about.

Go and learn what this means: "I desire mercy,
not sacrifice." For I have not come to
call the righteous, but sinners.
Matthew 9:13

Chicken Nugget

"The church is not a museum for saints but a hospital for sinners."   *Morton Kelsey*

"Grace strikes us when, year after year, the longed-for perfection does not appear, when the old compulsions reign within us as they have for decades, when despair destroys all joy and courage. Sometimes, at that moment, a wave of light breaks into our darkness, and is as though a voice were saying, 'You are accepted. You are accepted, accepted by that which is greater than you. . . .' If that happens to us, we experience grace."

Paul Tillich
From *Shaking the Foundations*

CHAPTER 41

Waddling through the Wilderness

by Susan Duke

Trading the comforts of city life for dirt roads and a ten-mile drive to the nearest convenience store took pure pioneer spirit—nothing conventional for us.

Once the plans for our log house were drawn out on freezer paper, we were ready for action. We found a supplier in Colorado where we could buy logs wholesale. Before calling in our order to the logging company, my husband, Harvey, figured the exact length the mill should cut each spruce log. Considering we were building a four-bedroom log home, this was quite a tedious task. But I had complete confidence in my husband's years of contracting experience. Only one problem remained: how to get the logs from Colorado to East Texas.

One afternoon, the phone rang, and I was surprised to hear Harvey's enthusiastic voice on the other end. "Honey," Harvey exclaimed, "I've got good news! I'm at the 76 Truck Stop, and I've just met and hired a trucker who's going to Colorado. He's agreed to bring our logs back on his truck."

"How in the world did you work that out?" I questioned.

"I felt like I should stop here and check to see if someone was going that direction. I overheard this guy saying he was bringing an empty truck back from Colorado."

It seemed every detail had almost supernaturally worked out—from selling our city home in just three short weeks to finding temporary quarters to live in, only a mile from our building site. A week later, the trucker, true to his word, brought the logs, dumped them on our wilderness land, and we were ready to start building. God had surely smiled on us.

Or so we thought.

Then it started raining, and raining, and raining—forty days and forty nights. (Or so it seemed!) With no water lines, septic tanks, or driveway to the building site, we were stuck until the weather cleared.

This also happened to be the year that the savings and loan crisis forced the building industry to near collapse in the state of Texas. Other successful contractors we knew were suddenly forced to move up north just to find work. Preoccupied with our building project, at first we were not alarmed or concerned. Harvey was grateful to have the extra time to build our house and thought he could hire some of his crew to help erect the log shell faster.

But one disaster followed another. The cost of building materials tripled in one month. The plumber we prepaid to do the plumbing flew the coop to parts unknown. After we had our driveway graded and spread with what we'd been told was railroad rock, it turned to tar-like mud. We became well acquainted with one of our neighbors who owned a tractor, having to ask him to pull us out of the mud more than once.

On our first night in the country, we were awakened by the obnoxious odor of a visiting skunk. We had been initiated into

"Wilderness Survival 101." Then, when it dawned on me that mailmen and trash men don't come this far into the woods, I began to wonder if we had somehow made a terrible mistake.

Little did we know that we had enrolled in a school of learning that would eventually earn us an honorary B.S.D. (Back Side of the Desert) degree and what would prove to be the most challenging, soul-searching years of our life.

We found ourselves in a bewildering predicament. Harvey had no work. Timing forced us to move from our temporary housing into our unfinished home prematurely. We started calling ourselves Job and Jobetta.

We felt trapped and isolated. Why had everything seemed to fall into place so perfectly when we made the decision to move? Now that we'd actually set our feet on our new homestead, we were suddenly forced to scramble for our most basic needs—not just on a daily basis, but hour by hour.

One day I looked into our pantry and realized that other than a few potatoes and onions, our cupboard was bare. I closed the door and prayed aloud, "God, what are we going to do? What are You trying to teach us?"

Instantly, a verse from the Bible came to my mind. "Give, and it will be given to you" (Luke 6:38 NKJV). I remember feeling almost angry as I quipped, "Well, Lord, we would if we had something to give." All I could think of were those potatoes and onions and wondered if God could possibly be asking me to give them.

About that time, Harvey came bounding through the back door and without thinking, I blurted, "Honey, I need you to take something to the people who are building the new house next door." Just days before, a family had moved their travel trailer to a building site across the creek.

I found a nice country basket, lined it with a bright red-checked napkin and carefully placed my offering of potatoes and onions inside. Harvey didn't question why I felt so compelled to send him next door with the basket, but he did look perplexed when he asked, "And just what am I supposed to say when I give them these vegetables?"

"I don't know," I stammered, "just say, 'Welcome to the neighborhood!'"

Although nothing had changed, I had a strange sense of peace as I watched Harvey lumber out the door to deliver the goods. As I prepared supper (potato soup, of course) I heard a car pull up in the driveway. The boy who came to the door politely introduced himself as the neighbor's son.

"Ma'am, you know those potatoes and onions you sent to my mom?" he asked. "Well, she really appreciated them and we'll use them. But we just finished moving out of our old house this afternoon and we had to clean out our freezer and cabinets. There isn't much room in the travel trailer, so my mom told me to just bring all this stuff in hopes maybe you can use it."

There on the porch next to his feet were four bulging grocery bags of frozen meats, vegetables, and canned goods—enough to last two weeks. He brought them in, I thanked him, and he went on his way.

As foolish as it seemed at the time, responding to the gentle nudge to share our potatoes and onions had quickly yielded an abundant harvest—manna from heaven.

Often Harvey and I felt the heat and the isolation of that dry season, but God illuminated our lives one moment at a time with the assurance of His presence, even when we felt confused and alone. Building a log home became secondary to building a foundation of confidence in God that could not be shaken by circumstances.

One day I looked up the word "wilderness" in a Bible dictionary and discovered the Hebrew word means "a place where God speaks to us and pastures us." My heart was filled with a settled peace. God had a plan.

While I would not care to relive the trials of those two seemingly endless years before the sun began to shine again, I would not trade our lessons learned in the wilderness.

Today, we enjoy the warmth, peace, and solitude of our beautiful log home in the East Texas woodlands. Many say they feel God's presence the moment they walk through its doors. It's a perfect setting in which to live and write.

Even woodland creatures are drawn to our haven for free meals. Ramona, a raccoon who has been visiting us at our back door every night for two years, now has the courage to walk right in when the door is left standing open. For a year, she's been bringing her three bashful babies, now full grown and thriving from the enormous amounts of cat food they devour nightly.

What treasures and blessings we have found growing among thorns of tribulation in the wilderness. Therefore, I rejoice in the confidence of knowing that even if I waddle through a wilderness, I am trusting God every step of the way.

*When you walk, your steps shall not be hampered
[your path will be clear and open]; and when you run,
you shall not stumble. Take firm hold of instruction,
do not let go; guard her, for she is your life.*
Proverbs 4:12,13 AMP

Everyday Survival Kit

Items Needed:

Toothpick, rubber band, bandage, pencil, eraser, chewing gum, mint

1. Toothpick—to remind you to pick out the good qualities in others (Matthew 7:1).

2. Rubber band—to remind you to be flexible, things might not always go the way you want, but it will work out (Romans 8:28).

3. Bandage—to remind you to heal hurt feelings, yours or someone else's (Colossians 3:12-14).

4. Pencil—to remind you to list your blessings every day (Ephesians 1:3).

5. Eraser—to remind you that everyone makes mistakes, and it's okay (Genesis 50:15-21).

6. Chewing gum—to remind you to stick with it and you can accomplish anything with Jesus (Philippians 4:13).

7. Mint—to remind you that you are worth a mint to your Heavenly Father (John 3:16,17).

Meet the Authors

Becky Freeman has a full nest with her hubby, Scott, and their four chicks. Her brood supplies much of the material for her books, which include *Worms in My Tea, Marriage 9-1-1, Still Lickin' the Spoon, A View from the Porch Swing,* and *Real Magnolias.*

Becky has been interviewed on more than three hundred radio stations and appeared on television programs such as *Good Morning, Texas* and *The Crook and Chase Show.* She also writes the popular, "Marriage 9-1-1" column for *Home Life Magazine.* Becky is popular as a humorous speaker across the nation.

Susan Duke is an author, motivational speaker, and singer. She ministers at Christian conferences, women's retreats, seminars, and churches of all denominations through her own "Heartsong Ministries." She has recorded several Gospel albums, and writes Gospel music, psalms, and poetry.

Susan coauthored *Heartlifters for Women* and *Heartlifters to Encourage and Inspire.* Her work has appeared in publications such as *Home Life, The Greenville Herald Banner, The Cross and the Quill,* and *Lifestream.* She makes her nest in a quaint log home built by her husband, Harvey. Susan received the award "First Time Conference Best Work Submitted" at the 1998 Florida writers' conference.

Rebecca Barlow Jordan, a full-time freelance writer, has published more than 1,500 greeting cards, articles, stories, and numerous calendars, including the 365-day *In His Image.* Her works have appeared in *Focus on the Family, Discipleship Journal, Home Life, Family Circle, Marriage Partnership,* and others. She coauthored *Marriage Toners: Weekly Exercises to Strengthen Your Relationship* with her husband, Larry, who is an associate pastor. Rebecca has also contributed to three other books.

Rebecca is a speaker for women's events and writers' conferences, and leads marriage enrichment weekends, banquets, and other marriage events with her husband. She has been a deaf interpreter, a newspaper columnist, and a Bible study teacher, and has won two American Christian Writers' Awards. She is a mother hen at rest in her emptied nest with two grown daughters.

Gracie Malone is a freelance writer, Bible study teacher, and conference and retreat speaker. For many years, she has mentored women, developed leaders, and established small group ministries and churches throughout the United States. Her articles have been published in *Discipleship Journal, Moody, Christian Parenting Today, Home Life, Women Alive, Decision,* and others. She received the "Best Article" award at Florida's Christian writers' conference.

Gracie and her husband, Joe, who is an engineer, have three sons and six grandchicks.

Fran Caffey Sandin is the author of *See You Later, Jeffrey,* and a contributing writer for *The Strength of a Woman.* Fran's numerous articles have appeared in *Moody, Virtue, Focus on the Family Physician, Home Life, Journal of Christian Nursing, The Christian Medical Society Journal, Aspire, Pray, Decision, The Joyful Woman,* and others.

Fran is a registered nurse and works for her husband, James, who is a physician. She is an organist in her church, codirects women's ministries, and teaches a young couples' class with her husband. They have three children: a single rooster, a married hen, and their youngest chick, who is waiting for them in heaven. They have recently become grandparents and find it delightful.

The Greenville Hens coauthored the first *Courage for the Chicken Hearted* in 1998.

A NOTE FROM THE EDITORS